Quick Guide

TRIM & MOLDING

CREATIVE HOMEOWNER PRESS®

COPYRIGHT © 1994
CREATIVE HOMEOWNER PRESS®
A Division of Federal Marketing Corp.
Upper Saddle River, NJ

Writer: Mark Feirer
Cover Design: Warren Ramezzana
Cover Illustrations: Brian Demeduk
Book Packager: Scharff Limited
Printed at: Quebecor Printing Inc.

Current Printing (last digit)
10 9 8 7 6 5 4 3 2

Quick Guide: Trim & Molding
LC: 93-073996
ISBN: 1-880029-27-8 (paper)

CREATIVE HOMEOWNER PRESS®
A Division of Federal Marketing Corp.
24 Park Way
Upper Saddle River, NJ 07458

C O N T E N T S

S A F E T Y   F I R S T

Though all the designs and methods in this book have been tested for safety, it is not possible to overstate the importance of using the safest construction methods possible. What follows are reminders; some do's and don'ts of basic carpentry. They are not substitutes for your own common sense.

- *Always* use caution, care, and good judgment when following the procedures described in this book.

- *Always* be sure that the electrical setup is safe; be sure that no circuit is overloaded, and that all power tools and electrical outlets are properly grounded. Do not use power tools in wet locations.

- *Always* read container labels on paints, solvents, and other products. Provide proper ventilation, and observe all other warnings.

- *Always* read the tool manufacturer's instructions for using a tool, especially the warnings.

- *Always* use a push stick when ripping narrow pieces on a table saw. Never cross-cut short pieces on a table saw.

- *Always* remove the key from any drill chuck (portable or press) before starting the drill.

- *Always* pay attention to a tool as you use it; avoid using a tool if you expect to be interrupted.

- *Always* know the limitations of your tools. Do not try to force them to do what they were not designed to do.

- *Always* make sure that any adjustment is locked before proceeding. For example, always check the rip fence on a table saw or the bevel adjustment on a portable saw before you use the tool.

- *Always* clamp a small workpiece to your work surface before drilling it.

- *Always* wear the appropriate gloves when the work calls for it. Use rubber gloves when handling masonry, moving lumber, or doing demolition work.

- *Always* wear a dust mask when working in a dusty environment. Wear the appropriate respirator when working in the vicinity of chemical vapors.

- *Always* secure the workpiece firmly when cutting it with a portable circular saw. Clamp it to a work surface if you can; this will allow you to keep both hands on the saw for maximum control.

- *Always* keep your hands away from the business ends of blades, cutters, and bits.

- *Never* work with tools when you are tired or under the influence of alcohol or drugs. Remember that many prescription and non-prescription drugs cause drowsiness.

- *Always* check your local building codes when planning new construction. The codes are intended to protect public safety—you should observe them to the letter.

- *Never* saw a workpiece that spans a large distance between supports without also supporting it on either side of the cut line; otherwise the piece will bend as you cut it and the pieces will pinch the blade. The saw will kick back toward you violently.

- *Never* cut very small pieces of wood or pipe. Cut only pieces large enough to clamp or hold securely.

- *Never* change a blade or a bit unless the power cord is unplugged. Do not depend on the switch being off; you might accidentally hit it.

- *Never* work in insufficient lighting.

- *Never* work while wearing loose clothing, hanging hair, open cuffs, or jewelry.

- *Never* work with dull tools. Have them professionally sharpened, or learn how to sharpen them yourself, using proper equipment.

- *Never* use a power tool on a workpiece that is not firmly supported or clamped.

- *Never* carry sharp or pointed tools, such as utility knives, awls, or chisels in your pockets. Instead, carry them in a tool belt with leather or heavy-canvas pockets.

- *Never* support a workpiece with your leg or other part of your body when sawing.

- *Always* wear eye protection, whether working with power tools, hand tools, or chemicals. A nail hit off center can ricochet off the wood and hurtle toward your face with blinding speed, and solvents can splash into unprotected eyes.

- *Always* clean up wood shavings and other debris before you start to trip over it.

CHOOSING TRIM & MOLDING

Trim and molding can be used to complement— or create—any architectural style from traditional to contemporary. By planning the job in advance, you can minimize problems and make the work go more smoothly.

Trim versus Molding

Trim and molding come in a variety of shapes, sizes, and species of wood. To begin with, however, let's clear up some confusion regarding terminology. You will find the words "trim" and "molding" used interchangeably, even by people who ought to know better. In fact, however, each term refers to a slightly different item. "Trim" is the name given to wood that is rectangular in cross section, with no embellishments. Trim is typically 1 inch thick or less. Part of the confusion is that the word "trim" is also used as a general description of any wood in a house that isn't structural lumber—baseboards, casing, even moldings. The professional who traditionally installs all this material, for example, is called a trim carpenter. The word "molding," on the other hand, refers specifically to thin strips of material, usually wood, that have been cut, shaped, or embossed in some way to create a decorative effect. Molding includes everything from simple quarter-rounds to elaborate crown molding.

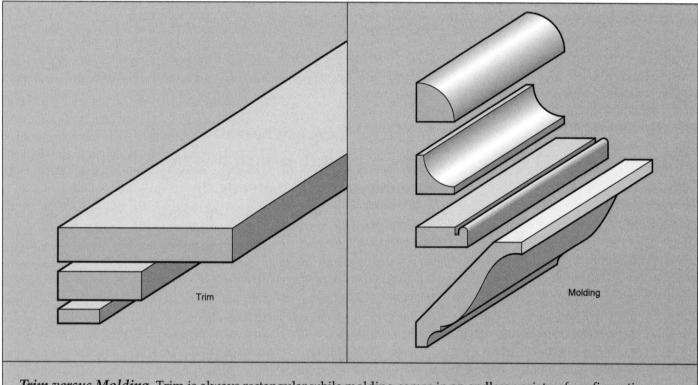

Trim versus Molding. Trim is always rectangular while molding comes in an endless variety of configurations.

Nailing Molding to the Wall

Molding comes in such a wide variety of profiles and thicknesses that it is difficult to give universal nailing recommendations. In general, however, nails should penetrate into a solid substrate. That means the nail should be long enough to go through the molding, through the drywall or plaster, and into the framing securely. For outdoor work, all nails should be hot-dipped, galvanized; indoors, uncoated steel nails are best.

To install large molding—crown, cove, baseboard, and chair rail—drive two finish nails into each stud. One nail should be about 1/2-inch from the bottom edge, the other 1/2-inch from the top. Small molding like base cap and quarter round need only one nail per stud. It's a good idea to keep three sizes of finish nails on hand: 4d, 6d, and 8d. When nailing near the end of a run of molding, predrill the nail holes to keep the wood from splitting and to make sure the nail goes where you want it to. Use a 5/64-inch bit for 4d nails, a 3/32-inch bit for 6d nails, and a 7/64-inch bit for 8d nails.

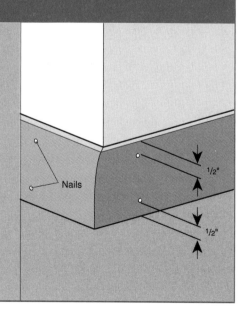

Nails

1/2"

1/2"

Purposes of Trim & Molding

To properly include trim and molding into the design of a house, you should consider both decorative and functional details. Though trim and molding are most often used decoratively, they are hardly without utility. In fact, they can be essential to preserving the structural integrity of a house by blocking the passage of water or protecting a surface against mechanical damage.

Used as a Barrier. Trim around the outside of a window or door, for example, bridges the gap between jamb and sheathing to keep water

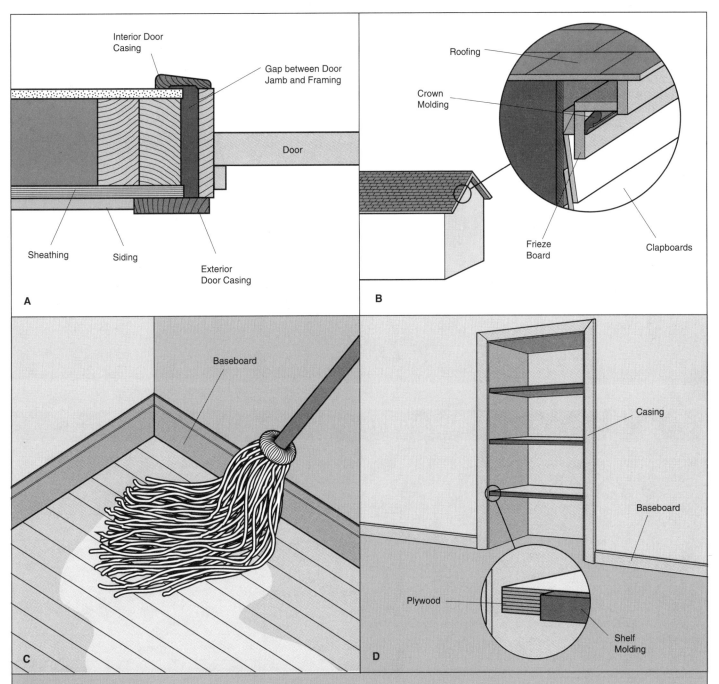

Used as a Barrier. (A) Trim or molding is often used to cover the inevitable gap where two or more materials meet. Door trim and window trim are the most common example of this. (B) This detail of crown molding and frieze board shows how trim and molding can be combined in a decorative detail that is also functional. (C) One reason baseboard is used to protect the lower portion of walls becomes clear when you consider baseboard's other name: mopboard. (D) Plywood makes good shelf material, but the exposed layers of veneer would soon become damaged if they were not covered with solid wood shelf molding.

out, while eaves molding closes the gap between roof and wall. Inside the house, baseboards protect walls just as shelf molding protects the edges of shelving.

Used as a Cover-up. Trim and molding can minimize problems caused by the natural movement of wood. Wood is inherently an unstable material; exposed to water or humidity it will swell, then it will shrink as heat or dry air drives the moisture out. Over time, this movement forms gaps that are more than unsightly: they can also collect dirt and debris. The proper application of molding won't stop the wood from moving, but it can eliminate the problems that it causes.

Used as a Decoration. When applied to a plain surface such as a flush door, for example, the added pattern and texture can make the door a lot more interesting. Crown molding serves a purely decorative purpose in dressing up the juncture of wall and ceiling, and draws the eye upward much as a church spire does.

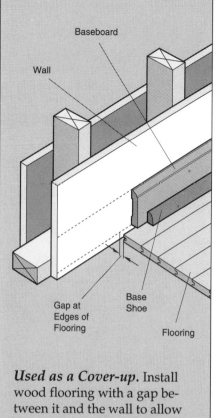

Used as a Cover-up. Install wood flooring with a gap between it and the wall to allow for movement. By nailing the baseboard and base shoe into the wall, the flooring is free to move.

Used as a Decoration. An inexpensive flat panel door can be transformed with molding and imagination. This door uses panel molding to mimic a panel door.

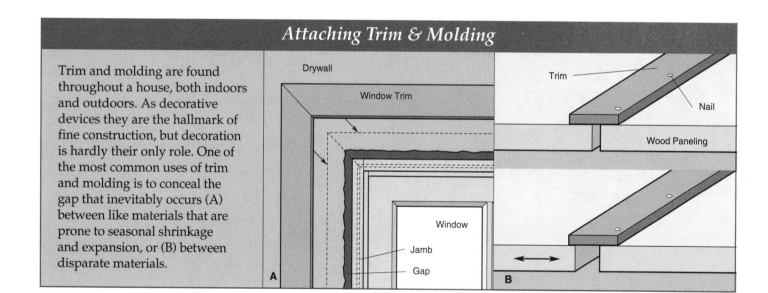

Attaching Trim & Molding

Trim and molding are found throughout a house, both indoors and outdoors. As decorative devices they are the hallmark of fine construction, but decoration is hardly their only role. One of the most common uses of trim and molding is to conceal the gap that inevitably occurs (A) between like materials that are prone to seasonal shrinkage and expansion, or (B) between disparate materials.

Design Principles

Trim and molding come in a considerable array of sizes and shapes, most of which can be used in many ways. Here are some guidelines for choosing patterns and profiles.

Stick with One Style. It is a rare room that can handle a smorgasbord of trim styles, so pick a style and stick with it. If you are adding trim to an existing room, match the existing trim. Take a few samples to the lumberyard to ensure a match—you might find a couple of lengths stashed in your attic or tucked away in your garage. If you're combining trim or molding, work with compatible shapes.

Watch the Intersections. In any room, various elements of trim or molding will intersect each other, such as where baseboard meets the door casing. The relative thicknesses and widths will determine if the elements meet harmoniously or awkwardly. Before you settle on a collection of trim, get actual samples

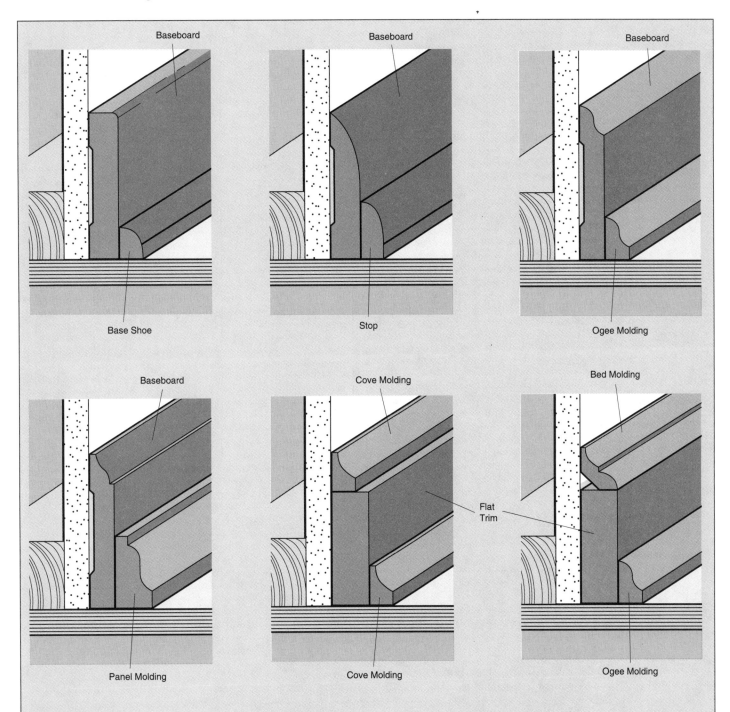

Stick with One Style. Even though these baseboards were built up using individual pieces, the profiles of each element are compatible with others in the same assembly.

(scraps will suffice) so you can examine the intersections in advance.

Think "Finishes" before Finishing. Staining trim usually makes it stand out; painting it to match surrounding surfaces helps it to blend in. Trim that contrasts with surrounding surfaces emphasizes its linear nature. Painted trim allows a greater margin of error; you can fill small gaps before you paint. Stained or clear-finished trim, on the other hand, will point out every mistake.

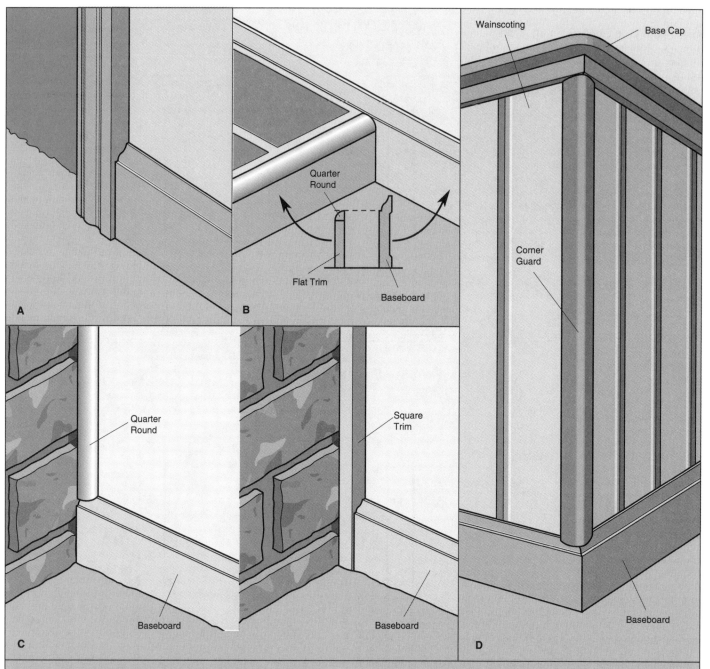

Watch the Intersections. (A) Here the outside edge of the door casing is thicker than the baseboard, so the two intersect nicely. If the reverse was true, the end grain of the baseboard would be exposed and form a rather clumsy-looking detail. (B) In this case, the flat trim and quarter-round used to cap a woodstove platform butts nicely into the side of the baseboard. If the quarter-round was instead an ogee, it might be an even better match. (C) These two trim elements don't even come close to blending nicely. A better solution would be to run square trim alongside the fireplace all the way to the floor, then butt the baseboard into it. (D) The corner guard meets the underside of the wainscoting cap in tolerable fashion. It meets the baseboard in a much more visible location, however, and in a much clumsier fashion.

Avoid Awkward Applications.
When it comes to applying trim or molding to angled features, such as sloped ceilings, the work gets complicated in a hurry—you'll have to make some tricky compound-angle cuts. Even then, the results may not look quite right, so it may be best to save your molding work for other parts of the room.

Use Classic Applications. Builders in classical Greece (who originated many of the profiles upon which modern moldings are based) realized that decorative moldings looked best when they were viewed head on. In this way, shadows wouldn't obscure the molding.

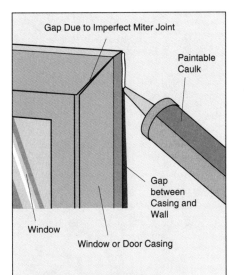

Gap Due to Imperfect Miter Joint

Paintable Caulk

Gap between Casing and Wall

Window

Window or Door Casing

Think "Finishes" before Finishing. You can use paintable caulk to hide any gaps in trim that will be painted. This is particularly useful where trim is being installed on a wall that's not perfectly flat.

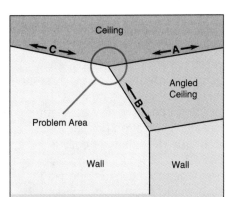

Ceiling

C

A

Angled Ceiling

B

Problem Area

Wall

Wall

Avoid Awkward Applications. The intersecting ceiling planes in this example would make the application of crown molding quite difficult. The crown molding couldn't follow the ceiling line "A" because of the obtuse angle it forms; following ceiling line "B" would result in an awkward intersection with any trim along ceiling line "C."

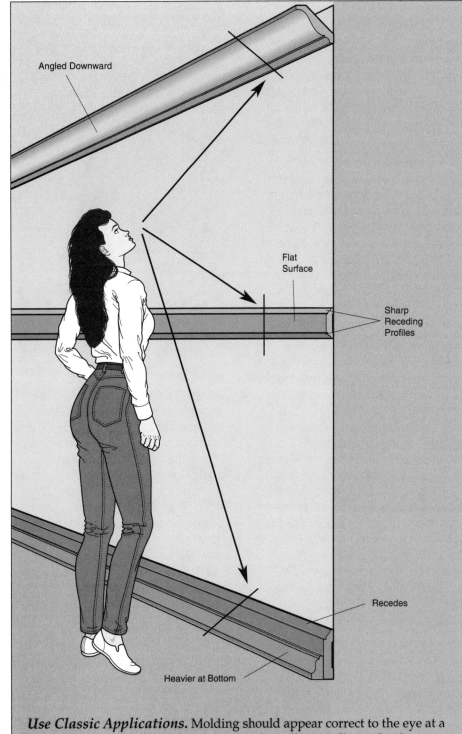

Angled Downward

Flat Surface

Sharp Receding Profiles

Recedes

Heavier at Bottom

Use Classic Applications. Molding should appear correct to the eye at a normal stance. Molding toward the top of a wall generally angles downward, while those at the bottom usually have a profile that is heavier at the bottom than at the top.

Grades of Trim & Molding

Trim and molding are available in various species of softwoods. The most commonly available are fir, pine, hemlock/fir, and spruce, though availability varies considerably from region to region. Softwoods are easy to cut, relatively inexpensive, and are readily stained or painted. When it comes to hardwood, most home centers and lumberyards carry only oak. Oak is more difficult to work with and considerably more expensive than any of the softwoods, but more durable.

Grading is a way of distinguishing one piece of wood from another in terms of its quality and its suitability for a particular purpose. It also has a considerable effect on the cost of wood. In order to control your costs, always purchase wood in the grade most suitable for the work you are doing. Buying a higher quality than you need entails needless expense.

The grading of trim is quite complicated, and terms used to describe various grades often vary from region to region. In general, however, trim is divided into appearance grades and general purpose grades. Each of these grades is further divided into numerous subcategories. Appearance grades are most suited for the high-quality finish uses, particularly indoors (though you may find that the best of the general purpose boards will suit your needs as well). In addition, you may also see trim stock referred to by the term "S4S" (surfaced four sides). This means both faces and both edges have been planed smooth.

When it comes to molding, there are only two basic grades: clear and paint-grade. Clear molding is made from solid lengths of high-quality wood and has no visible defects. This premium product can be painted or stained. Paint-grade molding is a relatively new product that consists of many small pieces of wood joined

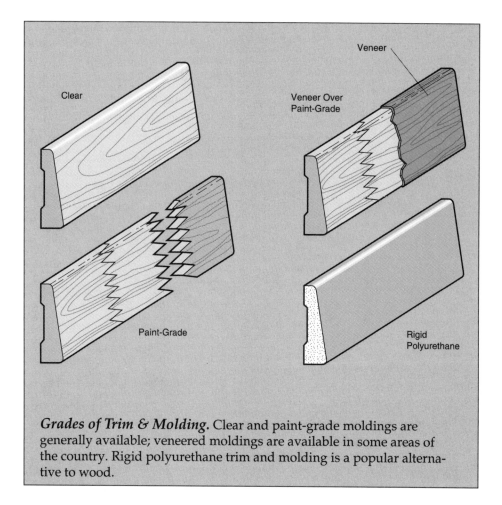

Grades of Trim & Molding. Clear and paint-grade moldings are generally available; veneered moldings are available in some areas of the country. Rigid polyurethane trim and molding is a popular alternative to wood.

together into one long piece using adhesives and interlocking joinery. This material is sometimes called "finger-jointed" stock, after the joinery method used to connect the pieces. The pieces themselves are good quality wood, but neighboring pieces often vary a great deal in color and grain. These differences are concealed when the molding is painted, however, making the finished product virtually indistinguishable from clear molding. As you might expect, paint-grade molding is less expensive than clear molding.

There is another grade of molding worth noting. Known by various trade names, it is essentially finger-jointed wood stock wrapped either with solid wood veneer or wood-grained vinyl. Both of these hybrid products can be cut with standard woodworking tools, and are nailed in place just like standard molding. However, you must take particular

care not to damage the thin outer layer during installation.

Wood isn't the only material used for molding, however. Some lumberyards carry molding made entirely of rigid, furniture-grade polyurethane that has a paintable coating. The molding comes in very detailed, classically-inspired profiles that would be difficult and costly to reproduce in wood. Rigid polyurethane is lightweight and very stable, and cuts can be made with a hand saw. The material is typically installed using a proprietary construction adhesive, with a few small nails here and there to hold lengths in place while the adhesive cures. Once painted, the molding is difficult to distinguish from solid wood. Polyurethane molding usually costs more than wood molding, but it will take a lot less time to install detailed profiles that you would have to build up with wood.

Buying Trim & Molding

For a relatively small project—casing a single window, perhaps—all you have to do is go to the lumberyard, buy a length or two of molding, then come home to install it. But large jobs are different; any new room could well require baseboard, chair rail, ceiling molding, base shoe, and casings for doors and windows. You will get the best price, and save yourself many trips to the supplier, if you purchase all your molding at the same time.

Because of the variations in grading around the country, it's best to visit your local supplier before ordering trim or molding. Ask to see samples of various grades—many suppliers keep samples on hand just for this purpose. Be sure to describe what you plan to do with the wood and how you expect to finish it; the supplier can often recommend less-expensive grades that will perform very well.

Checking for Deformities. The problems that plague framing lumber, such as warping and twisting, affect trim to a lesser extent and molding lesser still. This is because trim and molding are carefully dried before shipping, whereas lumber is often shipped "green." However, you should still pick material with care in order to identify any problems before you have to live with them. First, sight down the length of the wood; this will make it easy to see twisted or bowed stock. Usually a gradual bow in molding won't be much of a problem—the wood is thin enough to straighten out against the wall as you nail it into place. Then, scrutinize the molding for splits or any other damage.

Trim stock is thicker and usually wider than molding, so it won't conform as easily to the wall if it is bowed. (See "Trim versus Molding," page 6.) Even so, a slight bow is tolerable as long as it goes with the thickness of the board.

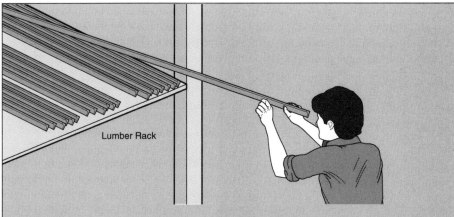

Buying Trim & Molding. Sight down the length of a piece of molding to determine if it is straight. A slight bowing is okay, but any twist will cause problems during installation.

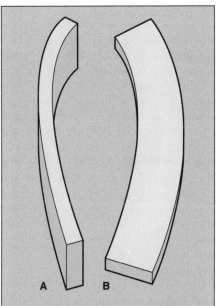

Checking for Deformities. A trim board (A) bowed across its thickness may be usable, but a board (B) bowed even slightly across its width will be difficult to work with.

Choosing the Stock. Because moldings come in lengths of 8 to16 feet, you should rarely need more than one piece to trim a given wall. If you're on a tight budget though, shorter pieces sometimes cost less than longer ones. The techniques used to mill moldings aren't perfect, so check any moldings that you buy for fractional differences in width and thickness. Whenever possible, buy all the molding for a project at

Storage Tips

Proper storage cannot be overemphasized. Trim and molding should always be stored indoors, preferably in the same space in which it will be installed. This allows it to acclimate to the moisture levels present in the room. Keep trim and molding away from all masonry walls and floors (particularly floors). These surfaces will wick harmful moisture into the house from the outside, and it's the moisture that can cause damage to the molding. Badly warped molding is unusable molding.

During the course of the project, make it a point to save any scrap molding that is 6 inches in length or more until the end of the job. You will often need some scraps to experiment on, such as when setting up test cuts. Also, you'll find that shorter pieces are useful as stock from which to cut small pieces called "mitered returns." (See "Mitered Returns," page 33.) Even after the job is complete, you should still save some scraps—they may come in handy later on if you have to make repairs.

one time to minimize any variations. Even a small variation in width can make an otherwise perfect joint look clumsy.

Estimating Molding Stock. Molding stock typically comes in lengths from 8 to 16 feet, but you can usually get shorter lengths if you ask (though you may have to pay extra if the lumberyard has to cut molding for you). Simply measure the amount you'll need, add about 10 percent to account for waste, and you're in business. Purchase the longest lengths of stock that you can transport; this will give you the most flexibility when it's time to cut the material to fit.

To figure out how much you'll need, measure each wall and round up the number to the next foot. In other words, a 5-foot 6-inch wall requires a 6-foot length of molding. To allow for cutting waste, each piece of molding for the wall should be longer than the wall it will cover. If the wall is almost the length of a full piece, buy the next longest length. That means ordering 8-foot lengths for a wall whose length is within an inch or two of 6 feet.

Estimating Trim Stock. Trim lumber typically comes in the widths as shown in the chart below. The nominal size is what you would ask for; the "actual" size is what it measures.

Trim Lumber Sizes	
Nominal size (in inches)	Actual size (in inches)
1x2	3/4 x 1 1/2
1x3	3/4 x 2 1/2
1x4	3/4 x 3 1/2
1x5	3/4 x 4 1/2
1x6	3/4 x 5 1/2
1x8	3/4 x 7 1/4
1x10	3/4 x 9 1/4
1x12	3/4 x 11 1/4

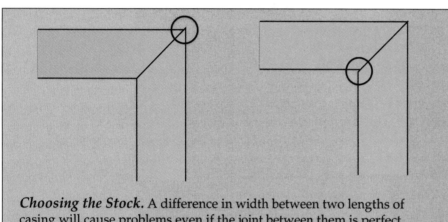

Choosing the Stock. A difference in width between two lengths of casing will cause problems even if the joint between them is perfect. On the left the "horn" resulting from differing casing widths can be sanded down. On the right, however, there's not much you can do about the unsightly gap.

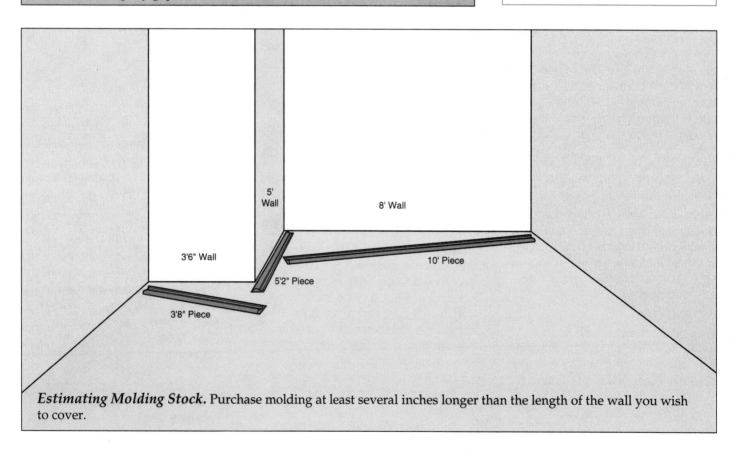

Estimating Molding Stock. Purchase molding at least several inches longer than the length of the wall you wish to cover.

Types of Molding

You will find that the molding bins are stuffed with every conceivable shape or profile of molding, and nearly every one of them is available in several dimensions.

Base Molding. Baseboard protects the lower portion of the walls, and covers any gaps between the wall and the floor. Base shoe molding is used to conceal any variation between the floor and the baseboard bottom. It is also used to cover edges of sheet vinyl flooring (when installed without first removing baseboard).

Ceiling Molding. Cove covers the inside corners between sheets of paneling. It is also used for built-up crown molding. Crown molding

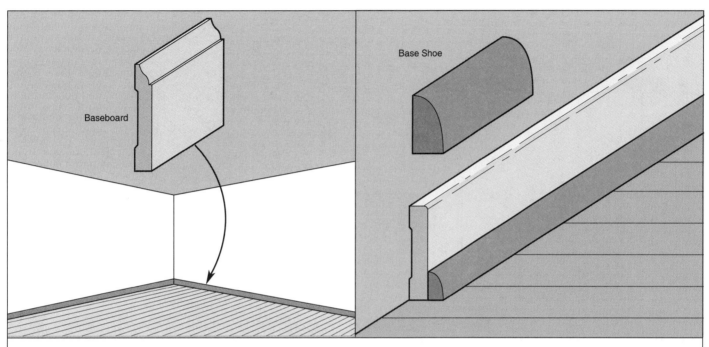

Base Molding. Baseboard protects the bottoms of walls and base shoe covers the edges of newly-installed flooring.

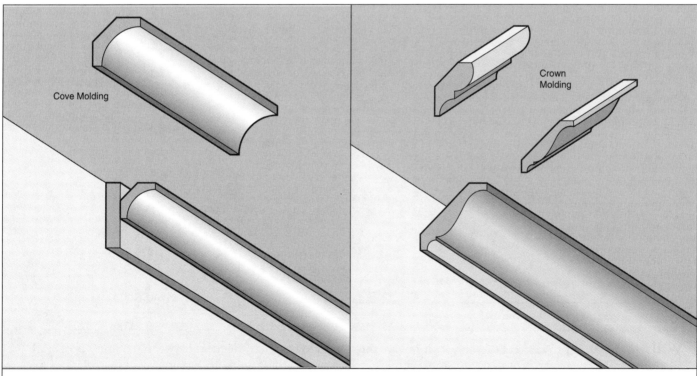

Ceiling Molding. At the intersection of the wall and ceiling, cove or crown molding is installed.

is used for dramatic effect at the juncture of walls and ceilings.

Wall Molding. Wainscot cap can be used to cover the exposed end grain on solid wood wainscoting, or to finish off the top of flat baseboards. Chair rail molding is installed at the height that protects walls from being damaged by chair backs. It is also used to cover the edges of wallpaper wainscoting. Picture rail is used in conjunction with metal hooks for hanging paintings. It eliminates the need to put holes in the wall. Corner guards protect the outside corners of drywall or plaster in high-traffic areas.

Casing. Casing conceals the gap between jambs and the surrounding wall. Common types of casing include Ranch, Clamshell, and Colonial. Mullion casing is used as

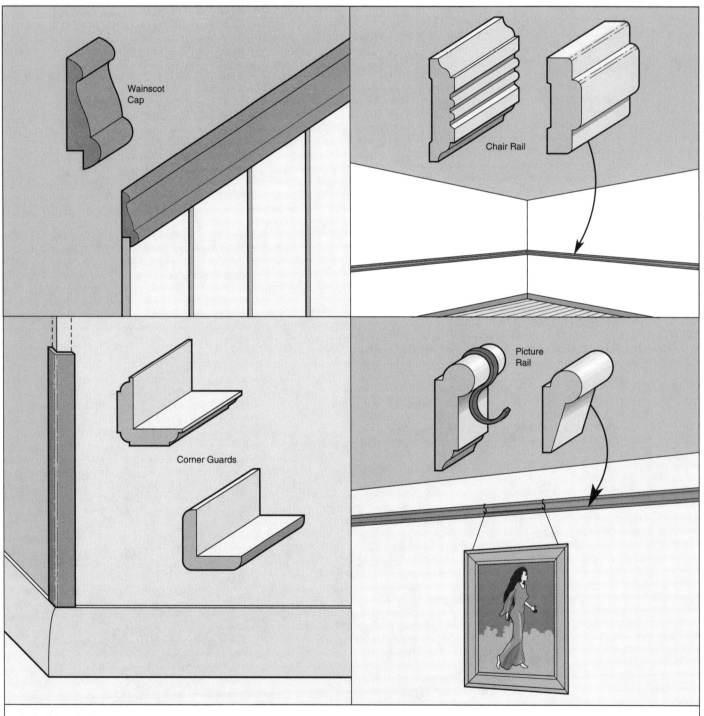

Wall Molding. (Top) Wainscot cap and chair rail are often used to bridge differences between materials on a wall. (Bottom left) Corner guards protect vulnerable corners from damage. (Bottom right) Picture rail allows pictures to be added, moved, and removed without marring wall surfaces.

the center trim between two or more closely spaced windows. Be sure it is compatible with the window casing in style and thickness. If you don't find a casing style that you like, you can make your own out of flat trim stock. Even a pair of 1/8-inch deep kerfs, cut lengthwise in the stock on a table saw, can add a dramatic detail.

Other. Back band molding can be used to give the outer edges of flat casing a more decorative profile. It can also be used as a base cap, or even as inexpensive stock for framing small artwork. Shelf molding covers the exposed edges of plywood or particleboard casework and shelving. This is an inexpensive way to give manufactured material the look of solid wood.

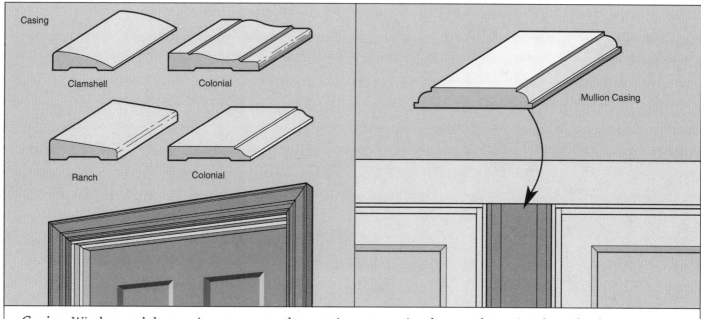

Casing. Window and door casing are among the most important trim elements for setting the style of a room.

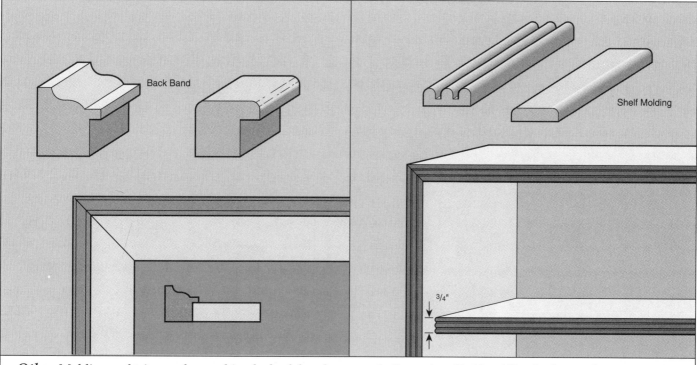

Other. Molding and trim can be combined—back band surrounds flat casing. Shelf molding is also used on casework.

Making Your Own Molding

While your local lumberyard probably stocks any molding profile you want in softwood or oak, you'll have a hard time finding moldings in walnut, cherry, or any other hardwood species you have in mind. But cherry stain doesn't really look like cherry wood and no matter what stain you put on oak, the grain will never look like walnut. For the real thing, you'll need to take out the router.

These days router bits are available in hundreds of decorative shapes. You can put a decorative edge on a piece of stock and use it as is. Or to make thin moldings, you can rip the decorative edge off the board and rout the board again, repeating this process so that one board serves as rough stock for several lengths of molding. By varying the depth of cut and combining different bits, even more profiles are possible.

Before using any router to cut custom molding profiles, be sure you know how to use the tool. Also remember that routers generate a great deal of sawdust and are very loud; protect your eyes and your hearing. Carbide-tipped router bits are more expensive than steel bits, but they keep a sharp edge longer and cut cleanly through nearly any wood.

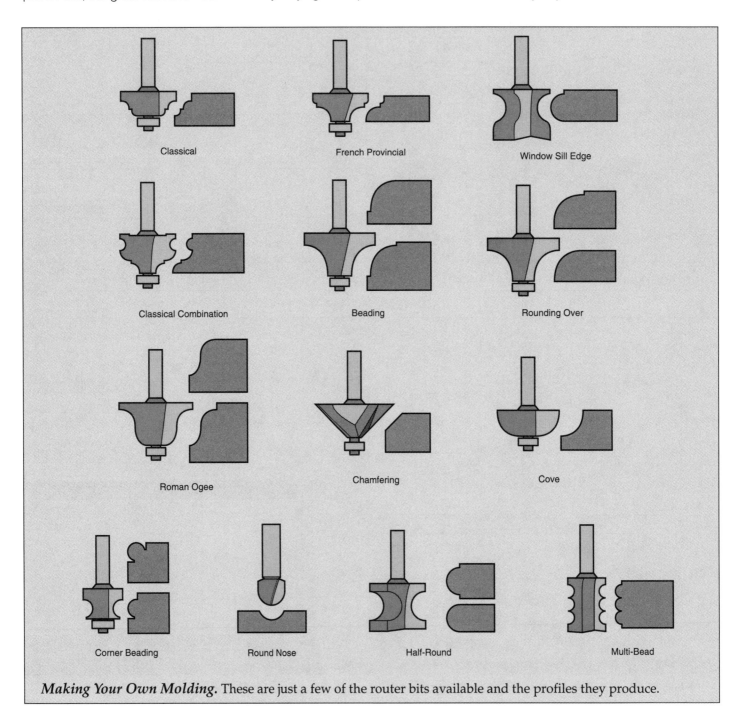

Classical

French Provincial

Window Sill Edge

Classical Combination

Beading

Rounding Over

Roman Ogee

Chamfering

Cove

Corner Beading

Round Nose

Half-Round

Multi-Bead

Making Your Own Molding. These are just a few of the router bits available and the profiles they produce.

Cutting Custom Profiles

1 Securing the Stock. First examine the board for knots, cracks, and other imperfections that would interfere with the cut. Tight knots that are small usually won't cause a problem, but you should avoid large or loose knots. Always clamp the stock to a solid surface so you can keep both hands on the router itself.

2 Adjusting the Depth of Cut. With the router unplugged and resting on top of the board, sight along the edge of the board. Adjust the height of the router bit, plug it in, and make a trial cut. (If you use scrap stock for this, it should be the same thickness as the final stock.)

3 Making the Cut. The router bit will spin clockwise. Guide it along the edge of the board as shown; the direction in which you work is important. Experiment with the rate of feed: too fast and you may damage the molding; too slow and the bit may leave burn marks on the wood. Multiple light passes will produce the cleanest edge with a minimum of burning.

4 Removing the Molding. If you are making molding, cut the routed edge from the board, set it aside, and then rout the fresh edge. You can continue to do this as long as you can safely clamp the stock in place while routing and safely cut it off on the table saw.

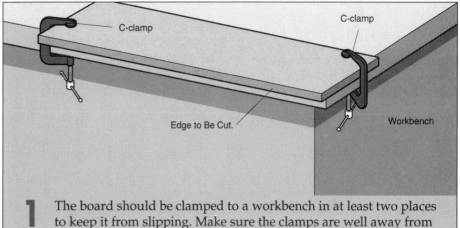

1 The board should be clamped to a workbench in at least two places to keep it from slipping. Make sure the clamps are well away from the edge to be cut, otherwise they will interfere with the router.

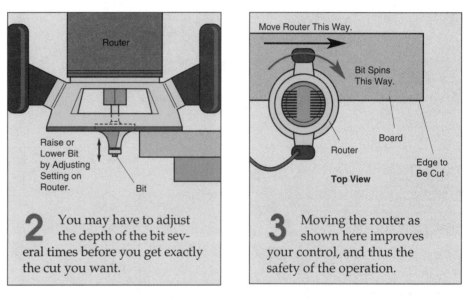

2 You may have to adjust the depth of the bit several times before you get exactly the cut you want.

3 Moving the router as shown here improves your control, and thus the safety of the operation.

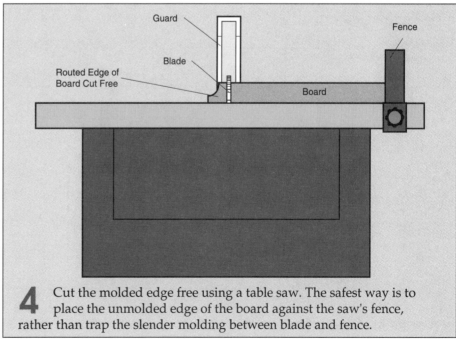

4 Cut the molded edge free using a table saw. The safest way is to place the unmolded edge of the board against the saw's fence, rather than trap the slender molding between blade and fence.

Assembling Custom Profiles

If a local supplier has a good selection of moldings, ask for some scraps and experiment with various combinations. When you find a suitable combination, you can either nail it in place piece by piece, or you can nail all the pieces together into lengths, then install the assembly just as you would any other molding. Once installed and painted, it will look just like solid stock. Get a price estimate on the molding, though, before you load up on enough of it to do a room; molding can be expensive, built-up molding even more so.

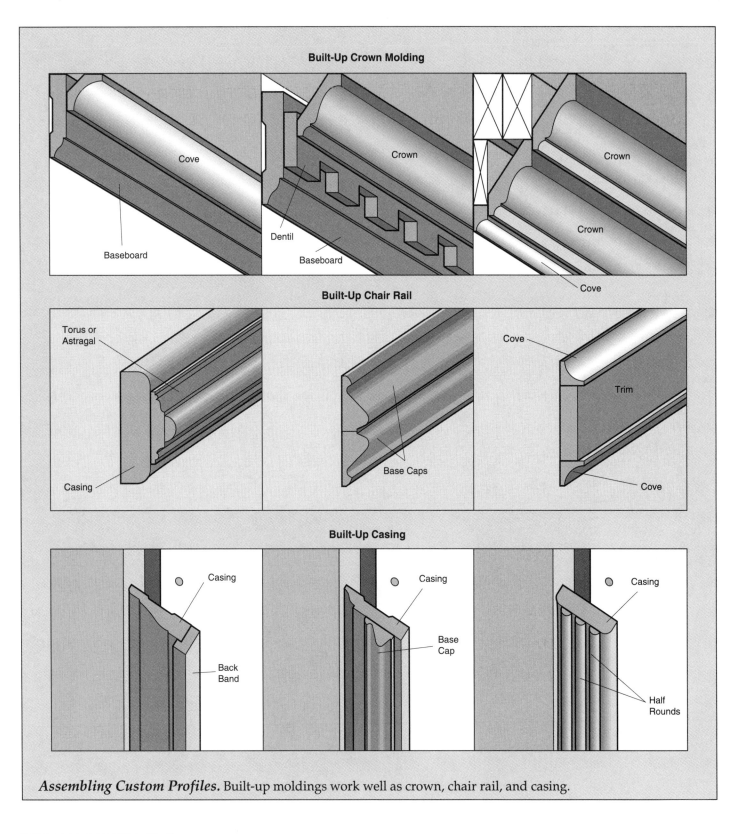

Built-Up Crown Molding

Cove
Baseboard

Dentil
Crown
Baseboard

Crown
Crown
Cove

Built-Up Chair Rail

Torus or Astragal
Casing

Base Caps

Cove
Trim
Cove

Built-Up Casing

Casing
Back Band

Casing
Base Cap

Casing
Half Rounds

Assembling Custom Profiles. Built-up moldings work well as crown, chair rail, and casing.

SELECTING & USING TOOLS

Though the work requires relatively few tools, installing trim and molding calls for more patience and closer tolerances than many other household projects. This is because the results of your work will be very visible— they might even be the focal point of a room—and any flaws will be readily apparent. Using the right tools for the job will help ensure handsome results.

Tools

To install trim and molding, you will need some basic tools. At the very least, you'll need a tape measure, hammer, hand saw, miter box, and some nail sets, along with a good, sharp pencil. These tools are widely available and relatively inexpensive.

Purchase additional tools as you need them. Power tools can improve the accuracy and speed of your work. Hand tools are perfectly suitable, however, particularly if you work with trim and molding only occasionally.

Tools

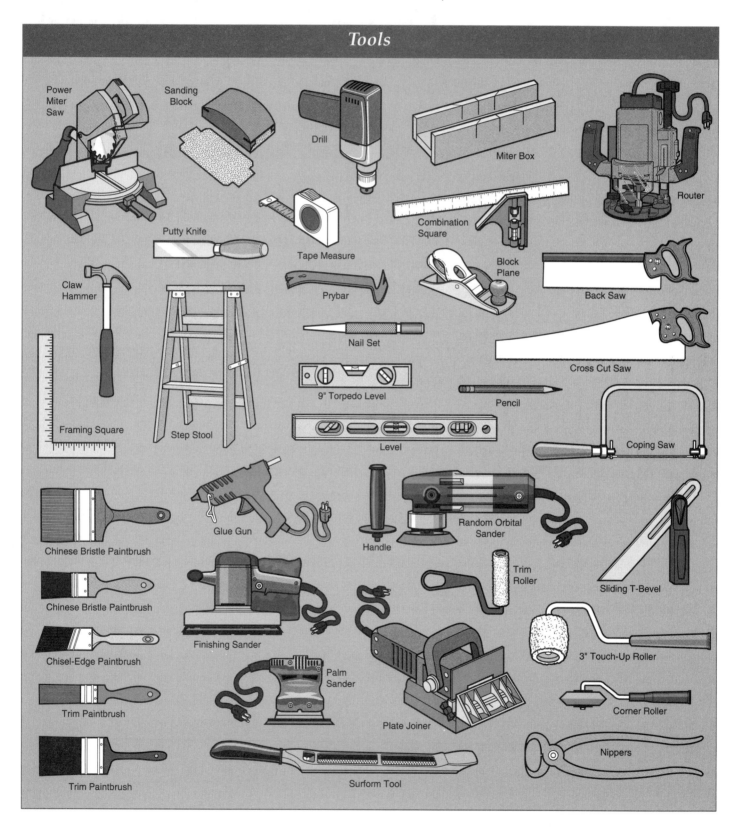

Power Miter Saw

Sanding Block

Drill

Miter Box

Router

Putty Knife

Tape Measure

Combination Square

Block Plane

Back Saw

Claw Hammer

Prybar

Nail Set

Cross Cut Saw

Framing Square

Step Stool

9" Torpedo Level

Pencil

Level

Coping Saw

Chinese Bristle Paintbrush

Glue Gun

Handle

Random Orbital Sander

Trim Roller

Sliding T-Bevel

Chinese Bristle Paintbrush

Finishing Sander

3" Touch-Up Roller

Chisel-Edge Paintbrush

Palm Sander

Corner Roller

Trim Paintbrush

Plate Joiner

Nippers

Trim Paintbrush

Surform Tool

Using a Tape Measure

A tape measure is a simple device, but it is easy to use improperly. Here are some tips for getting the best results with this important tool.

Checking for Accuracy. Any tape measure can be damaged if dropped, so check your tape periodically for accuracy (even a new one should be checked before you use it for the first time). The hook at the end of the blade slides back and forth just enough to account for its own thickness when you take inside or outside measurements; a bent hook, or one that does not slide, will give you inaccurate measurements. To check its accuracy, hook the tape on the edge of a board and make a mark at the 12-inch line. Now measure the same distance using only the graduated marks printed on the tape itself. Hold the 1-inch mark on the edge of the board, then measure out to your previous mark; it should fall exactly at the number 13. Carpenters sometimes call this process "burning an inch." If the measurements don't match, carefully bend the hook as needed until they do.

Making Measurements. To ensure an accurate measurement, always be sure that the tape is flat against the surface you're measuring. This is especially important when measuring long, flexible pieces of molding.

If you have to make a long inside measurement (the distance between two opposite walls, for example), hook the tape on a small finish nail tapped into the corner. The small hole remaining after you remove the nail will rarely be noticed.

Using the Small Slot. Have you ever looked at the hook of a tape measure and wondered what the small slot is for? It allows you to hook the tape on the head of a common nail and single-handedly make long measurements. With the nail serving as a pivot point, you can also use the tape measure to draw circles.

Maintenance & Care. A spring-loaded tape returns to its case quickly, but you should never let it snap back at full speed because this will eventually break the end of the tape. Instead, hold a finger under the tape so you can slow it down as it retracts. Periodically, wipe dirt and grime off of the tape, especially around the hook. If the tape itself breaks, you may be able to purchase a replacement cartridge for less than the cost of an entire new tape measure.

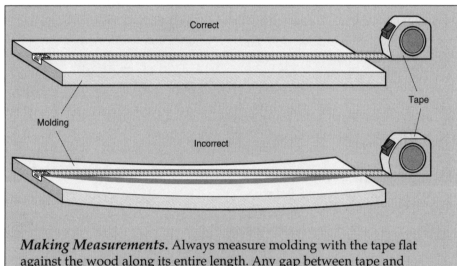

Making Measurements. Always measure molding with the tape flat against the wood along its entire length. Any gap between tape and wood will lead to inaccurate measurements.

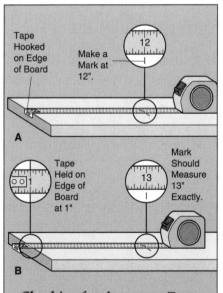

Checking for Accuracy. Test the accuracy of a tape measure by measuring to a mark both (A) with and (B) without using the hook. They should match.

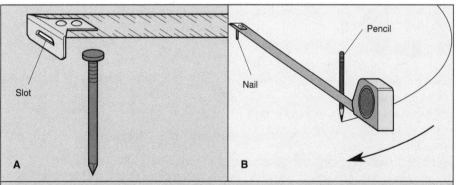

Using the Small Slot. (A) The slot in the end of a tape measure will fit over the head of a common nail to keep the tape from slipping as you measure away from the nail. (B) To lay out a rough circle, nail into a surface, hook the tape on the nail, then hold a pencil against the tape and swing a series of arcs.

Using a Hammer

A hammer can cause serious injury if used improperly. But, it is an indispensible tool if used properly when installing trim and molding.

Saving Time. You'll move around the room a lot while installing trim and molding. Much of your time will be spent looking for your hammer unless you keep it ready at your side. You can purchase a webbed belt with a leather pad and metal hanger for the hammer, or simply slip the hammer into the loop of an inexpensive canvas nail apron. Either way, your hammer will always be at hand when you need it.

Removing a Nail. Finish nails have a small head that a hammer can't always hold. It may help to bend the nail slightly so that the claws can get a better grip. If you are working with softwood trim or molding, slip a thin scrap of wood or heavy cardboard under the hammer head before you pull the nail; this will keep the wood fibers from being crushed as you lever the nail out.

Holding Small Nails. Here's how to minimize damage to your fingers when starting small nails. Hold them between two fingers (your fingernails toward the wood) as shown; your fingers will be flat against the wood rather than be angled upward, where the hammer might hit them. When space is really tight, you can hold the nails with needle-nose pliers or even with a piece of cardboard.

Setting a Nail. Nails used for installing trim and molding are shorter and thinner than those used in frame carpentry, and will bend easily if you're not careful. To start a nail, hold it in place and tap it lightly a couple of times until it stands by itself. Move your hand away and tap the nail harder until it is solidly engaged in the wood, then harder still as you drive it into the wood. Stop hammering just as the nail head reaches the wood; finish the job with a hammer and nail set. This will keep you from dimpling the wood as you drive the nail home.

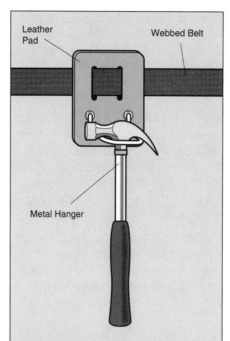

Leather Pad

Webbed Belt

Metal Hanger

Saving Time. This configuration is an ideal way to keep a hammer close by when you're not using it. The leather pad can be slipped onto a standard leather belt, too.

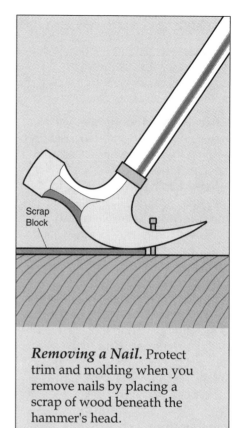

Scrap Block

Removing a Nail. Protect trim and molding when you remove nails by placing a scrap of wood beneath the hammer's head.

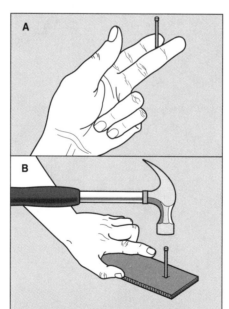

A

B

Holding Small Nails. (A) Hold a small nail with your palm up. Once the nail has started, move your hand away. (B) Very small nails can be held safely by first pushing them into a scrap of cardboard; hold the cardboard with your fingers well away from potential hammer blows.

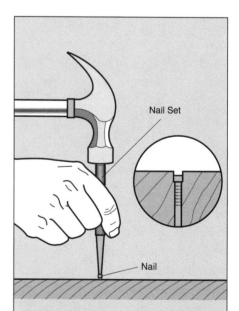

Nail Set

Nail

Setting a Nail. Hold a nail set by pressing its knurled barrel between your fingers and your thumb. Spread your fingers out slightly to stabilize the nail set, hold it against the nail, and tap it just below the surface of the wood.

Using a Power Miter Saw

The easiest and most accurate way to cut molding is with a power miter saw (sometimes called a chop saw because of the downward motion of the blade during cutting). Most power miter saws essentially consist of a circular saw that hangs from a hinged arm over an adjustable table and a stationary fence. The saw pivots left and right to make cuts of various angles. Power miter saws are especially accurate at removing thin slivers of material, which is often required to fit a molding precisely into place. To make the extra-clean cuts needed for molding work, fit the saw with a sharp, 60-tooth to 80-tooth carbide-tipped blade. The primary limitation of power miter saws is that they can't cut wide boards, but most trim and molding are easily accommodated.

Minimizing Problems. Like any power tool, a power miter saw can be dangerous if used improperly. Consult and follow the instructions that come with the saw, and wear both eye and ear protection. In particular, be careful when cutting molding. The pliable nature of thin stock encourages many operators to hold their fingers too close to the blade when cutting; a dangerous habit. Make sure to hold the stock firmly against the fence and flat against the table. The long length and slender profile of moldings such as small coves and base shoe makes them awkward to cut. To minimize problems, support all molding along its entire length.

Making Test Cuts. If you have never used a power miter saw before, make a number of test cuts on scrap stock to get accustomed to the cutting action. Because the saw blade must be aligned with the cut line by eye, it can be hard to get accurate results the first time. Try this approach. Pivot the saw down so that the blade's teeth almost touch the wood. (For safety's sake, keep your fingers away from the saw's trigger so you won't start the saw accidentally.) Then use the teeth as a guide to determine exactly where the saw will cut. After pivoting the saw back up and away from the wood, turn on the saw, and bring the blade down into the workpiece to make the cut.

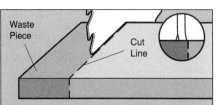

Making Test Cuts. Sight down the saw blade and line it up so that its teeth are completely on the "waste" side of the cut line. A proper cut will leave the line intact on the "good" piece, which you can always trim if your cut is slightly long the first time.

Using a Coping Saw

A coping saw has a steel frame and a narrow, flexible blade about 6 inches long, with 12 to 18 teeth per inch. The blade is held in tension between the "jaws" of the frame. Twisting the handle while you cut rotates the blade. This twisting gives the coping saw the ability to cut small-radius curves, making it possible to cut the profile of almost any piece of molding.

Start the coping saw by drawing it back gently over the cut line so that the teeth just barely cut into the wood. Continue to use short, gentle strokes until the blade begins to "track" in the cut, then use longer and firmer strokes.

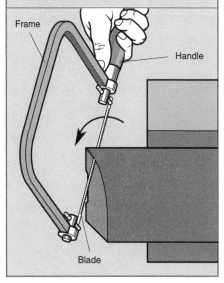

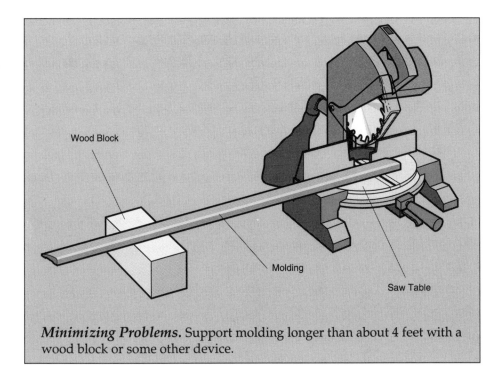

Minimizing Problems. Support molding longer than about 4 feet with a wood block or some other device.

Using a Miter Box & Back Saw

Even though the power miter saw has become universally popular among professionals, the wooden or plastic miter box still has its place. If you're cutting just a few pieces of molding, for instance, it may be easier to use a hand saw and miter box. And if you have to cut short pieces of molding, or if you're at all nervous about using a power saw, a wooden miter box is the best tool to use. Slots in the side of the miter box guide the saw blade, and allow you to make cross-cuts and 45-degree miter cuts (the cuts you will most often need). You can use the miter box with a back saw or with a standard carpenter's hand saw, as long as the saw is sharp. The more teeth per inch, the cleaner the cut will be. Sometimes miter boxes are metal, and hold the saw in a frame that minimizes wobble. Some of these saws can make compound miters, and some can even handle unusually wide stock. To make a cut, use your free hand to hold the stock firmly against the back of the box. Position your body so that your arm travels in line with the saw. Keep a light but firm grip on the handle and make the cut using a smooth, easy motion. To keep the cut smooth, don't bear down on the saw; the weight of the saw itself should carry it through the work.

Removing Slivers. Fitting a piece of molding often means shortening it by a fraction of an inch. Such a narrow cut can be difficult to make using a wood miter box because the saw blade tends to wobble off the cut line. To remedy this problem, take some scrap stock and tack it to the bottom of the box at the cut line. The block will serve as a guide to keep the saw blade straight.

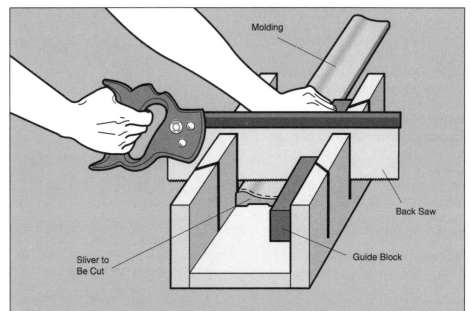

Using a Miter Box & Back Saw. Wooden miter boxes are inexpensive, and ideal when cutting short pieces of molding. One advantage of wooden miter boxes is that you can easily attach jigs to help you make a cut. A guide block, for example, allows the saw to remove a sliver from the end of a molding without wandering off the cut.

Using a Level

A small level (or two) is good to have on hand during trim jobs, though you probably won't use it a lot. Here are some tips for getting the best results with any level.

Reading a Level. First, set the level on the surface you wish to check, making sure the surface is free of sawdust and other debris. Your level may have either one or two sets of lines scribed into the circumference of each vial. Sight straight at the horizontal vial with one eye closed. (A) If the bubble is centered between the inner (or only) lines, the surface is level. (B) If you can see the lines on the back side of the vial, you're not looking straight at it. If one end of the bubble just touches one of the outer lines, this means the surface is sloping at a rate of 1/4 inch per foot (the rate at which plumbers slope drain lines). Some levels have one vial that is angled; when the bubble is centered in this vial, the level is sloping at a 45-degree angle.

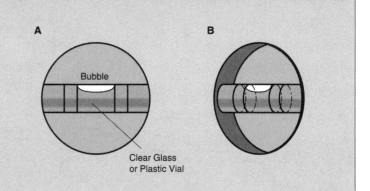

Checking Accuracy. An accurate level will read exactly the same if you turn it end for end on the same surface. If it does not, loosen the screws that hold each vial in place and adjust the vials until they read accurately.

Nails

Though you may occasionally need to use adhesives when installing trim and molding, nails are the fastener of choice—they're strong, inexpensive, and easily concealed with a dab of wood putty. Three types of nails are commonly used to install trim and molding: finish nails, casing nails, and brads.

Finish Nails. This is by far the most common type of nail used to install trim and molding. In fact, it is just about the only nail you need for this kind of work. The nail is characterized by a small, barrel-shaped head and a slender shank. The head, which has a small dimple in the top, is small enough so that you can use a nail set to sink it below the surface of the wood; this technique is called "countersinking." Finish nails are used whenever the nail must be concealed in the final work.

Casing Nails. A casing nail is similar to a finish nail, though the underside of its head is tapered. A casing nail has a bit more holding power than a finish nail of similar length; this is because its diameter is slightly greater than that of a finish nail. The extra holding power comes in handy when you install exterior casing, which is typically thicker than interior casing. Instead, it is simply driven flush with the surface of the wood and painted over. Not every supplier carries casing nails, however.

Brads. Nails shaped like finish nails, but less than 1 inch long, are called

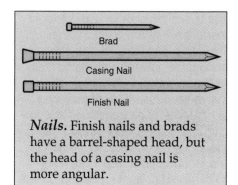

Nails. Finish nails and brads have a barrel-shaped head, but the head of a casing nail is more angular.

brads. They are used for tacking thin pieces of trim or molding into place.

Buying Nails. Finish nails and casing nails are available either uncoated or galvanized. Uncoated nails (often labeled "bright" for their shiny steel finish) are suitable for most interior work. Galvanized nails, on the other

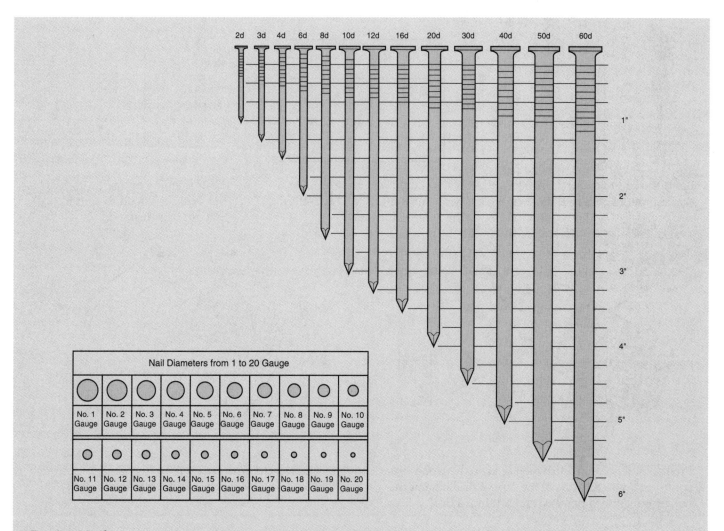

Buying Nails. Use this chart to determine the sizes and lengths of finish, casing, and standard nails.

hand, are the ones to use outdoors because they are coated with a rust-inhibiting layer of zinc. You can easily recognize galvanized nails by their dull gray color. Sometimes you'll see galvanized nails described further by the type of process used to apply the zinc coating: "hot-dipped" nails generally have a heavier coating of zinc than do "electroplated" nails. Galvanized nails are also appropriate indoors to fasten wood that may come into contact with moisture, such as any trim around a shower stall.

How you buy nails depends partly on where you buy them. The hardware section of a department store, for example, will sell small quantities in plastic packets holding a mere handful of nails each. Nails are cheap, but this is the most expensive way to buy them; use it only when your needs are minimal. At a home supply center or lumberyard, however, you'll also find nails in small boxes holding from 1 to 5 pounds each, or in bins that allow you to purchase nails by the pound in whatever quantity you want. The boxes provide a handy way to store unused nails so they'll be ready for the next project.

Sizes of Nails. Nails were once a precious commodity because each one was made by hand. Modern manufacturing makes nails relatively cheap, but our system of describing the length of nails harkens back to those early days. Nails are given a number, followed by a lowercase letter "d." The "d" represents the word "penny," which in turn refers to the fact that nails were once categorized by how much it cost to buy 100 of them. These days, however, the "d" represents the length of a nail, not its cost. A 2d nail (pronounced "2 penny"), for example, is 1 inch long, while a 60d nail is 6 inches long. Any nail less than 1 inch long is described by its actual length. You will rarely need a finish or casing nail longer than 16d (approximately 3½ inches).

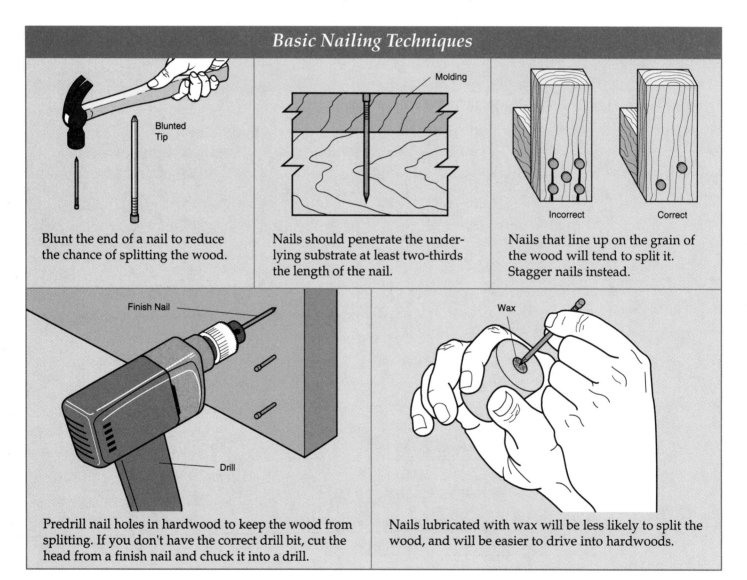

Basic Nailing Techniques

Blunt the end of a nail to reduce the chance of splitting the wood.

Nails should penetrate the underlying substrate at least two-thirds the length of the nail.

Nails that line up on the grain of the wood will tend to split it. Stagger nails instead.

Predrill nail holes in hardwood to keep the wood from splitting. If you don't have the correct drill bit, cut the head from a finish nail and chuck it into a drill.

Nails lubricated with wax will be less likely to split the wood, and will be easier to drive into hardwoods.

INSTALLING TRIM & MOLDING

Trim and molding is used throughout a house in countless ways. The techniques used to cut, fit, and install it, however, are relatively few. Once you understand these techniques, you can apply them to any trim or molding you buy or make.

Cutting Molding

Chances are you'll have to make at least one cut on every piece of molding you install. Unlike other areas of woodworking, where the joints may be structural, the installation of molding (indoors, anyway) is primarily decorative. That means that you can put your effort into making sure the installation looks good, with tightly fitting joints and no gaps between wall and molding. If you can master three basic kinds of cuts, your molding will be well on its way. The basic types of cuts are:

■ **Cross-cut**. This is usually the easiest cut for beginners to make. Sometimes called a square cut, it is simply a straight cut that runs across the grain of the wood. The grain of trim and molding runs along the length of the wood, so a typical cross-cut is across the width of the wood (90 degrees to its edges).

■ **Coped cut.** In some joints, one piece of wood must be cut to form a reverse image of the adjoining piece. The resulting cut may require a series of smaller cuts, each of which can be straight or curved. This is called a coped cut.

■ **Miter cut.** Like cross-cuts, miter cuts run straight across the grain of the wood, but at an angle other than 90 degrees. Miter cuts of 45 degrees are the most common because two pieces cut at this angle mate to form a 90-degree turn.

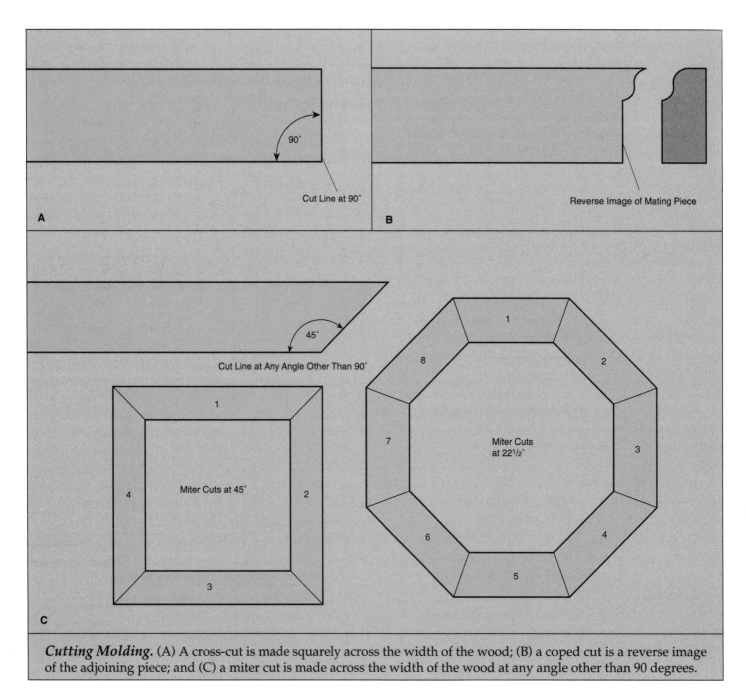

Cutting Molding. (A) A cross-cut is made squarely across the width of the wood; (B) a coped cut is a reverse image of the adjoining piece; and (C) a miter cut is made across the width of the wood at any angle other than 90 degrees.

Woodworking Joinery for Molding

How do you choose which joint to use when two lengths of molding meet? In general, every woodworking joint is a trade-off between strength, appearance, and your ability to use the tools. When installing molding, appearance is usually more important than strength.

Butt Joint. The simple butt joint is a 90-degree cut across the grain of a molding. It's often used where a length of molding meets a piece of standing (vertical) trim, such as where baseboard meets a door casing. A butt joint is easy to make, though for a tight fit it must be accurately cut— it must meet the vertical trim at a perfect right angle—and have a straight, smooth edge that's free of splintering. Any deviation from this will show up as an unsightly gap either at the top or at the bottom of the joint.

Miter Joint. Miters are made by cutting two pieces of molding at an angle and joining them—most commonly at the outside corner where two walls meet or around windows and doors (see pages 53 to 70). They're the most visible joints in most rooms, so you should take care when cutting and fitting them. Cut carefully because any deviation from your set angle will be doubled when two cut pieces meet. Miter joints look neat when you first cut them but can sometimes open up with changes in the wood's moisture content. A little glue and a casing nail can be used to close such a gap.

Coped Joint. If you use a miter joint on an inside corner, the joint will open up when you nail the adjoining pieces. It will open further as the wood shrinks with changes in moisture content. The solution is to use a coped joint. This is like a butt joint, except that one piece is cut to fit the profile of the other. Though a coped joint can also open up as the wood shrinks, any gap that results is less obvious than an equal gap in a mitered joint. In other words, a mitered joint accentuates a gap while a coped joint conceals it. Cutting a coped joint is not very difficult, and it even looks good when the corner isn't square.

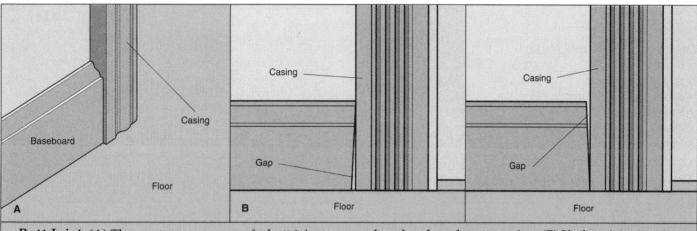

Butt Joint. (A) The most common use of a butt joint occurs where baseboard meets casing. (B) If a butt joint is cut at any angle other than exactly 90 degrees, a gap will show up against the casing.

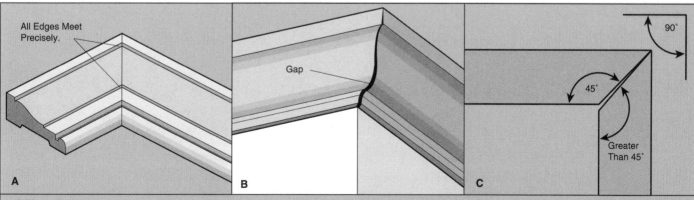

Miter Joint. (A) In a properly-cut miter joint, all edges and surfaces of the two pieces will intersect precisely at the miter. (B) One sign of a poor miter joint is a small gap at the outside of the joint. (C) Another sign of a poor miter joint is a misalignment of mating pieces. This sometimes happens when one piece is cut at an angle slightly different from that of the other piece.

Trimming a Miter

Using a Block Plane. Because many wall corners aren't exactly square, the ends of a miter joint must sometimes be trimmed with a block plane in order to make a perfect fit. When trimming a miter that doesn't fit exactly, remove wood from the back side of the cut until the front edges meet. To avoid chipping the front edges of the molding, trim the molding by removing material from the back side as shown.

Making Off-Angle Cuts. To miter moldings for a non-standard corner, you'll have to bisect the angle. The easy way to do this is to draw layout lines parallel to each wall and about a foot away from them. Then use a sliding T-bevel to copy the angle so you can transfer it to your power miter saw or miter box.

Miters on Non-Plumb Walls. Unfortunately, not all walls are precisely plumb (vertical), either. If the corner leans out, the top edge of the wall molding will be tight but a gap will show at the bottom of the molding. You might be able to live with this flaw on a baseboard—moldings at foot level aren't as closely scrutinized as others—but on ceiling molding the flaw will be visually obnoxious. Fix it by cutting a compound miter. Or, if an outside miter is open just slightly, you may be able to close it by burnishing the corner with a nail set.

Using a Power Miter Saw or Miter Box. You can make more accurate fitting adjustments by using a power miter saw or miter box.

■ Correcting a Corner That Is More Than 90 Degrees. To bring them together, cut angle "A" slightly less than 45 degrees, and retry the fit. If it still doesn't fit, recut angle "B" in the same way. Repeat the process until you have a tight fit.

■ Correcting a Corner That Is Less Than 90 Degrees. Cut the angle a little more than 45 degrees. One problem here is that most power miter saws

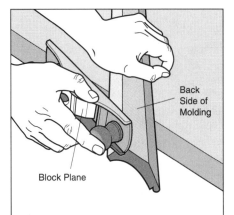

Using a Block Plane. When trimming a miter that doesn't fit exactly, remove some wood from the back side of the cut until the front edges meet.

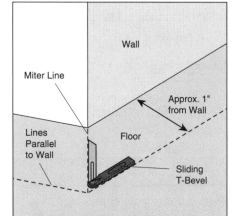

Making Off-Angle Cuts. Draw a line from the corner of the wall to the corner of your layout lines and use a sliding T-bevel to transfer the angle.

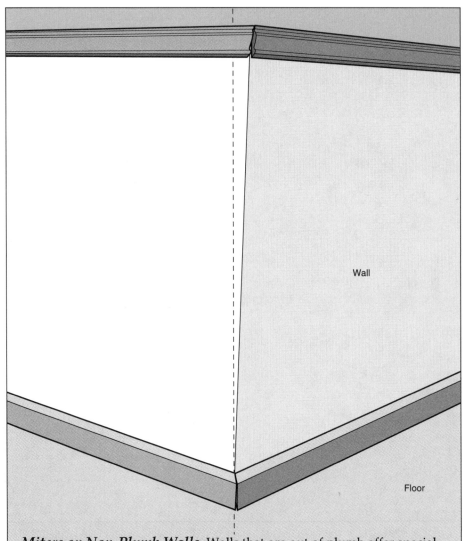

Miters on Non-Plumb Walls. Walls that are out of plumb offer special problems when molding must meet at a corner. Unless you make a compound miter cut, the joint will not fit properly. Be sure to start at outside corners, if any, to prevent pieces being cut too short when adjusting.

and miter boxes only make cuts up to 45 degrees. If you want to cut a steeper angle, you'll have to place a shim between the molding and the saw fence.

Mitered Returns. When a piece of molding (such as baseboard) terminates on a wall without meeting another molding, you can simply cross-cut it to length. However, this will expose the end grain of the wood, which is difficult to paint. A neater solution is called a "mitered return." The end of baseboard is mitered, then a small piece of matching molding is mitered and used to cap the end of the baseboard.

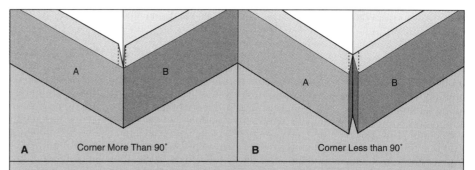

Using a Power Miter Saw or Miter Box. (A) To adjust the fit of a baseboard miter, cut angle "A" slightly less than 45 degrees. If the fit still isn't tight, do the same with angle "B." (B) To cut an angle of more than 45 degrees on some power miter saws, you may have to place a small shim between the workpiece and the saw fence. The angle of cut will increase depending on the thickness of the shim. Always start with outside corners, if any, to prevent a short measure at other end of piece.

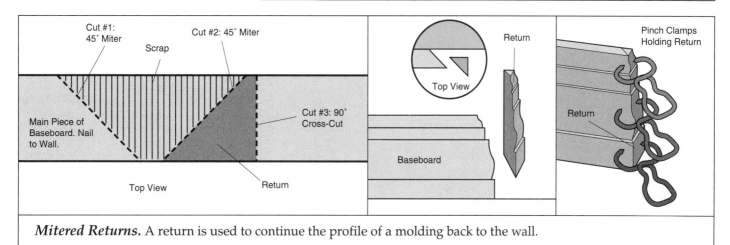

Mitered Returns. A return is used to continue the profile of a molding back to the wall.

Cutting a Compound Miter

A compound miter is a cut that angles in two directions simultaneously. (A) The cut end is 45 degrees to the edge and 30 degrees to the face of the wood, in this case. Only com- pound miter saws can make this kind of cut, and figuring out the specific angles can be tricky. (B) Rather than try to figure out all the angles to make a compound miter cut, simply use a wooden miter box and a shim to make the cut. Shim the top of the miter box so that the baseboard leans against it at the same angle as the wall angle, then make the miter cut.

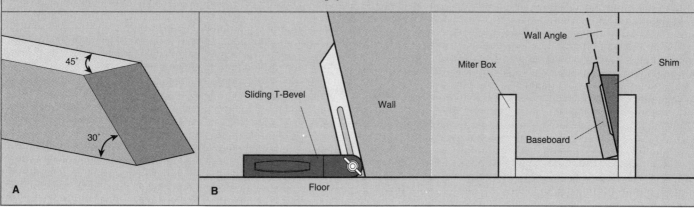

Coping a Baseboard

Cutting a coped joint is not difficult, but it does call for careful work and a dash of patience. The value of the coped joint, as opposed to a miter, is that it won't as easily show a gap if the molding shrinks slightly.

1 Installing the First Piece. Cross-cut the first piece of molding and butt it into the corner.

2 Making a Miter Cut. Cut a 45-degree miter on the intersecting piece of baseboard.

3 Cutting with a Coping Saw. Then use a coping saw to cut along the front edge of the miter.

4 Making the 90° Cut. Remove excess molding at the bottom to form a 90° angle. Test the fit by slipping the coped piece into place against the first piece of molding.

5 Making Trim Cuts. Use a round file or utility knife to fine-tune the back side of the cut. Retest the fit until you are happy with it.

6 Installing the Second Piece. The two cuts should produce a face that fits the contours of the piece to which it is butted.

Even a baseboard with a very simple profile should be coped for the best fit. Note that where the two pieces meet at the top edge, a very fine piece of wood will overlap from the coped piece to the butted piece. Take care during installation not to damage this fragile point.

For a tight fit, molding that is coped should be cut a bit long and then "sprung" into place. You'll have to experiment a bit to find out how much spring your molding has, and therefore how much longer to make it. Cut properly, the molding will snap into place with light pressure. If you have to force the molding into place, however, it's too long and will probably push adjacent molding out of position.

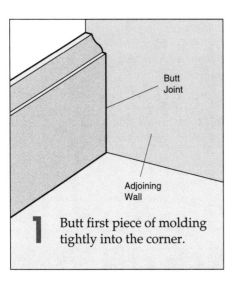

Butt Joint

Adjoining Wall

1 Butt first piece of molding tightly into the corner.

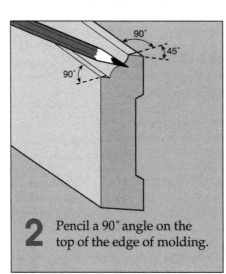

90°   90°   45°

2 Pencil a 90° angle on the top of the edge of molding.

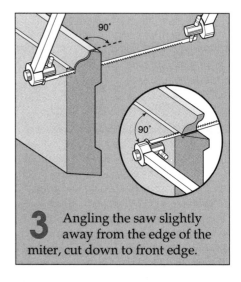

90°   90°

3 Angling the saw slightly away from the edge of the miter, cut down to front edge.

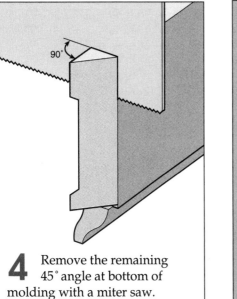

90°

4 Remove the remaining 45° angle at bottom of molding with a miter saw.

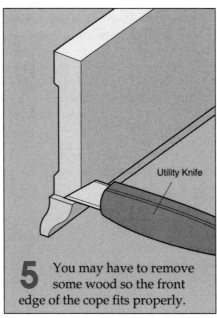

Utility Knife

5 You may have to remove some wood so the front edge of the cope fits properly.

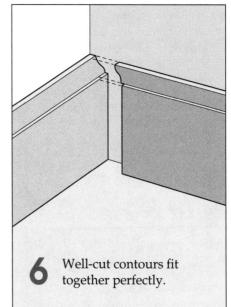

6 Well-cut contours fit together perfectly.

Making a Scarf Joint

A scarf joint is used to join lengths of molding end to end. Though moldings typically come in lengths long enough to cover a wall in one piece, this won't always be the case, particularly if you're trying to make the most of the molding you have on hand. A scarf joint is made by mitering the ends of two pieces of molding in opposite directions, then overlapping them. When joined, the overlapping pieces combine to make a flush surface. This joint is preferable to a butt joint because it won't show an obvious gap if the wood shrinks slightly in length.

The joint should occur over a wall stud whenever possible. This will allow you to nail through the joint and into the stud for a strong connection. Nails should be driven at an angle so that they fasten both splices to the stud.

1. Cut a 45-degree miter on molding #2 and nail the molding in place. Get an approximate measurement for molding #1, find a piece several inches longer than you need, then cut a 45-degree miter on one end, as shown. Test-fit the second piece, and cross-cut it to final length.

2. Nail through the top of the scarf joint and into a stud. Angle the nail slightly so that you can countersink the nail without pushing it clear through the top length of molding.

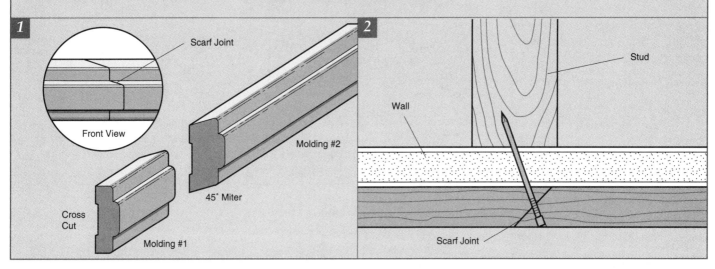

Cutting Picture Rail Molding

Picture rail is a ceiling molding that's installed somewhat differently than cove molding and crown molding. If the rail will actually be used to support heavy pictures (as opposed to serving a purely decorative function), it should be fastened to the wall studs with 2-inch long drywall screws. This will prevent it from pulling loose under the accumulated weight of many pictures. Also unlike crown and cove, picture rail need not be cut upside down. Instead, cut it exactly as it would lie on the wall. Picture rail is generally mitered on both inside and outside corners; it is not usually coped.

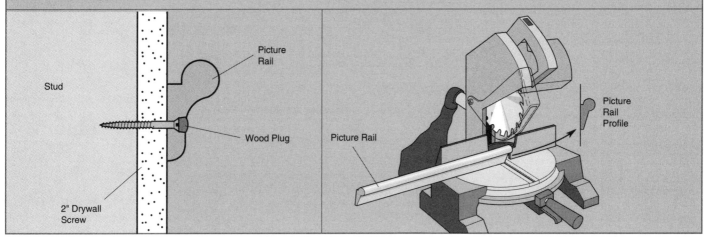

Strengthening Joints

Two effective methods of strengthening joints are incorporating wood blocking and biscuits.

Adding Blocking

Even the tightest of joints won't last very long if you don't nail into something solid behind it. If you plan ahead, you can add blocking to a wall as it is being framed. For instance, chair rail can be nailed to 2x4 stock nailed between the studs or to 1x4 stock recessed into notches cut into the studs. In either case, make sure the stock is securely face nailed or toenailed into place to provide a solid nailing surface to which the molding can be attached.

Installing Biscuits

A problem with butt and miter joints is that they can open up as the wood shrinks. One way to eliminate this problem is to join molding with wood splines called "biscuits." Biscuits are football-shaped pieces of compressed wood, and fit into a semi-circular cut made by a special tool called a plate joiner. Use white or yellow woodworker's glue to install biscuits; the glue makes the biscuit expand slightly, which makes the joint extra-strong.

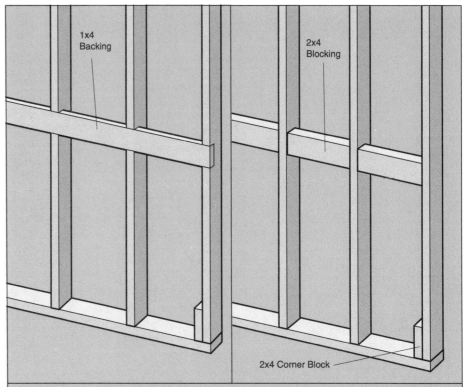

Adding Blocking. Add 1x4 or 2x4 stock to the wall as it is being framed to provide additional support to molding. A block at the corner of the wall provides extra nailing surface for the ends of baseboards.

1 Marking the Molding. Use a pencil to mark the two sides of the cut.

2 Marking the Slots. Line up the centerline of the plate joiner with the layout marks on the trim and make a slot in each side of the joint.

3 Securing the Joint. Glue a biscuit into the slots with white or yellow woodworker's glue and bring the joint together.

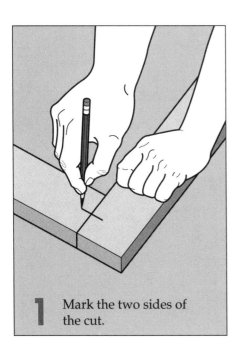

1 Mark the two sides of the cut.

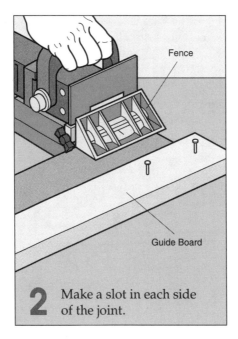

2 Make a slot in each side of the joint.

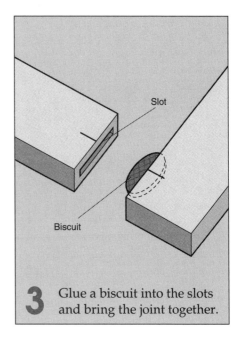

3 Glue a biscuit into the slots and bring the joint together.

Finding Studs

If you will be installing molding in an existing home, be ready to spend some time searching for studs. The most reliable method is to use an electronic stud finder. This hand-held device, which you can buy at most hardware stores, finds the framing behind the wall surface by measuring changes in the wall's density. You can also use a magnetic stud finder that "homes in" on the nails holding the drywall to the studs.

If you don't have either type of stud finder, you can sink finish nails into the wall until you hit a stud. In most houses, subsequent framing members will be spaced every 16 inches (centerline to centerline) from that point. You can also drill a small hole in the wall and probe through it with a stiff wire until you hit a stud. Then hold the wire where it penetrates the wall, pull it out, and use it to measure the distance to the stud. This usually works only on uninsulated interior walls, however.

Another trick is a simple one: by shining a light at raking angles over a wall, you can sometimes see telltale dimples over each nail where the patching compound shrunk. Finally, you can use a makeshift stud finder to find studs by first locating the nails used to secure drywall to them. Slowly pass a magnet over the wall surface; where it "grabs" there's a nail. Locate several nails to verify the location of the stud.

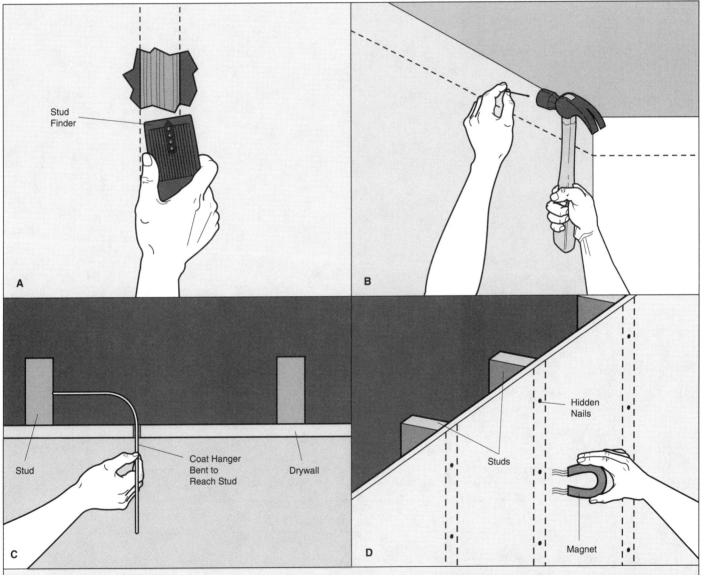

Finding Studs. (A) Using a stud finder is a simple matter of pressing a button and slowly dragging the device across the wall. A series of lights come on to show you the edge and the center of each stud or joist. (B) When probing for studs with a nail, work where the resulting nail holes will be covered by the molding you plan to install. (C) You can sometimes locate studs by probing through the wall with a stiff wire. (D) If you can find the nails used to attach the drywall, you'll know where the studs are. A magnet is the tool to use.

Installing Ceiling Molding

Like many projects, installing ceiling molding begins with some planning.

The idea is to figure out which joints will be coped, which will be mitered, and which will simply butt to the wall. If your walls are unusually long, you'll have to splice two shorter pieces with a scarf joint. (See "Making a Scarf Joint," page 35.) Your layout plans should note where that joint will go (over which stud, in other words).

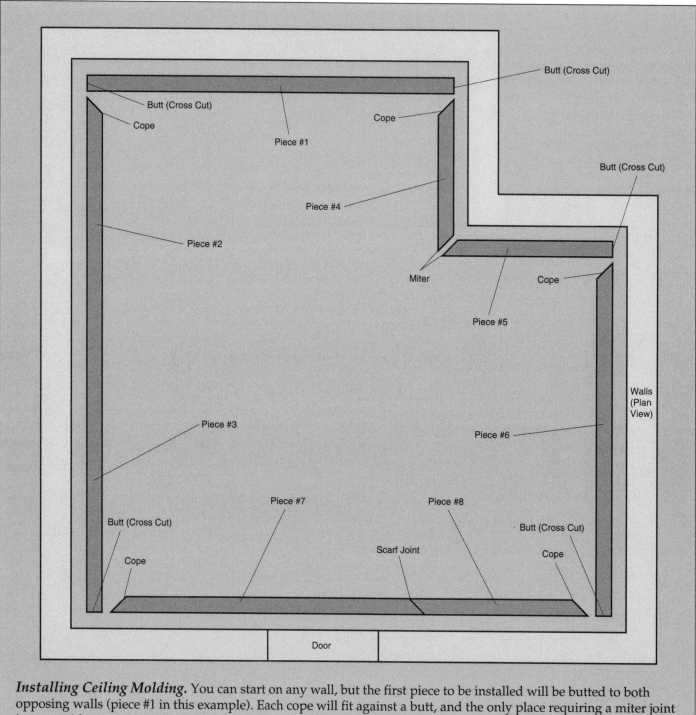

Butt (Cross Cut)
Butt (Cross Cut)
Cope
Cope
Piece #1
Butt (Cross Cut)
Piece #4
Piece #2
Miter
Cope
Piece #5
Walls (Plan View)
Piece #3
Piece #6
Piece #7
Piece #8
Butt (Cross Cut)
Scarf Joint
Butt (Cross Cut)
Cope
Cope
Door

Installing Ceiling Molding. You can start on any wall, but the first piece to be installed will be butted to both opposing walls (piece #1 in this example). Each cope will fit against a butt, and the only place requiring a miter joint is on outside corners.

Measuring for Ceiling Molding

You should also get a rough idea of the lengths of molding you'll need. Measuring for ceiling molding can be difficult to do single-handedly because nobody is there to hold the other end of the tape measure for you. There are several ways to get around this minor problem, however. The easiest is also the simplest; use a nail to hold one end of the tape. The hole will probably be covered later on by the molding, but if not you can always dab it with a bit of paintable caulk to make it disappear.

Sometimes it's tricky to get an exact measurement between walls, however, because the tape measure won't fit tightly into a corner. You can use a combination square to give the tape a more accurate "reach," or you can replace the tape altogether with two lengths of straight stock as shown.

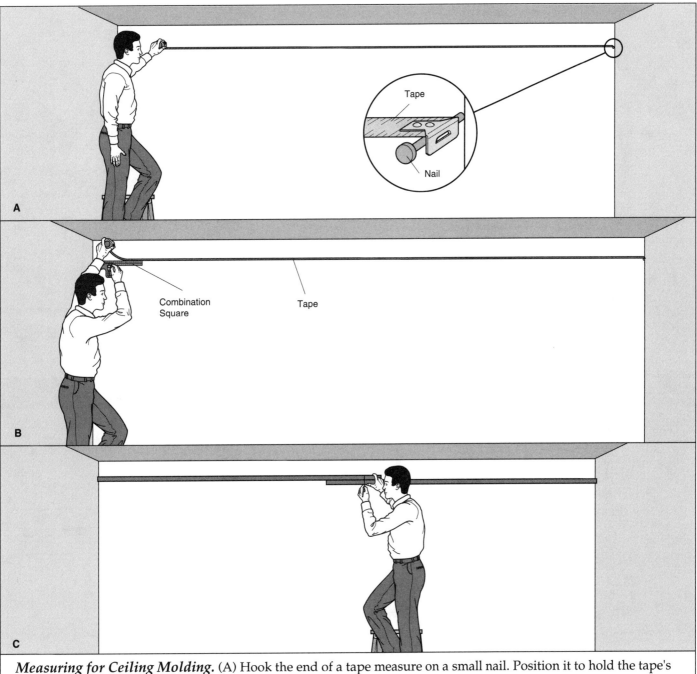

Measuring for Ceiling Molding. (A) Hook the end of a tape measure on a small nail. Position it to hold the tape's hook close to the wall and ceiling. (B) To get an accurate reading in a corner, "extend" it with a combination square. Add the length of the blade to your measurement. (C) Measuring sticks can be used when working solo. Slip them to each wall and make a mark where they overlap. Lay the sticks out on the floor (with marks lined up) and measure the total length with your tape.

Vaulted Ceilings & Molding

Standard ceiling molding won't fit properly where surfaces meet at other than 90 degrees, as where a vaulted ceiling meets the wall. Use window casing instead.

1 Duplicate the angle between the wall and the ceiling by using a sliding T-bevel as the cutting guide.

2 Transfer the angle to the cutting edge of the casing, making sure marking ends exactly at top front corner of casing.

3 Cut the casing with a table saw. Overcut the angle slightly to ensure that the casing edge will meet the ceiling exactly.

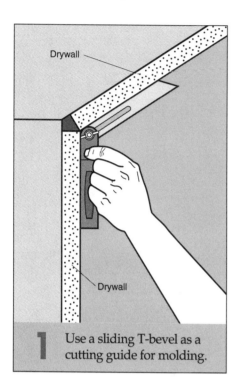

Drywall

Drywall

1 Use a sliding T-bevel as a cutting guide for molding.

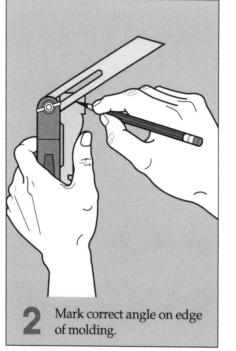

2 Mark correct angle on edge of molding.

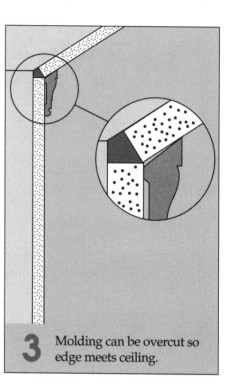

3 Molding can be overcut so edge meets ceiling.

When to Install Trim & Molding

Whether you're remodeling an older home or building a new one, the installation of trim and molding comes near the end of the project. Exterior trimwork goes on just before the house is painted. Indoor trimwork can be installed anytime after interior wall surfaces are complete and the joints (in the case of drywall) are taped. Be sure that drywall joints are smoothly tapered before you begin the trim, otherwise gaps will show behind any trim that crosses a joint, such as ceiling molding and the top edges of baseboard and chair rail.

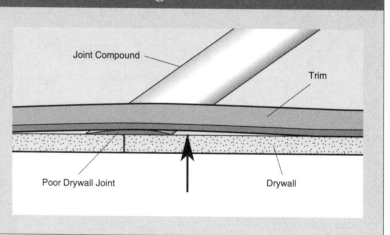

Joint Compound

Trim

Poor Drywall Joint

Drywall

Installing Crown Molding

Crown molding has a reputation for being difficult to install. But while installing crown is a bit more complicated than installing other moldings, it's certainly within reach of most do-it-yourselfers. The joints required are standard ones: butt, cope, and miter. The trick is to take the work a step at a time. The first step is to mark some layout lines on the wall. The method shown accounts for any imperfections in a ceiling that is not perfectly level.

Marking Layout Lines

1 **Measuring for Crown Molding.** With the tongue and the blade of a framing square representing the wall and the ceiling respectively, hold a piece of crown molding as shown to determine how far below the ceiling its bottom edge will be. Call this distance "A."

2 **Drawing Reference Line.** Draw a level reference line on the wall a few inches below this point. A long level is the best tool to use, though you may prefer to snap a chalk line.

3 **Finding the Low Point.** Measure up to the ceiling at various points in the room to find it's low point. Make a mark at distance "A" below this point. Measure up to this mark from your reference line. Do the same around the room's perimeter. Snap a second line at this height.

4 **Installing the Molding.** The molding's bottom edge must line up with this second line and nail the top edge directly up into the ceiling joists. Any remaining small gaps can be filled with drywall compound or paintable caulk.

If the ceiling is out of level, a level molding will highlight the problem and will leave a too-large gap between the top of the molding and the ceiling. In these cases, it's better to install the molding parallel to the ceiling. This will, however, complicate the fitting of joints.

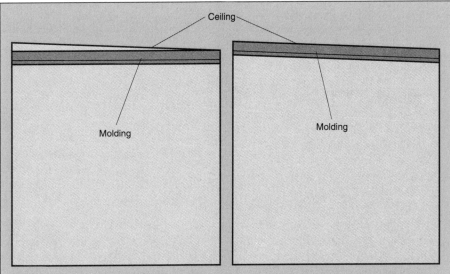

Marking Layout Lines. A level molding can sometimes accentuate the problem of a ceiling that is not level. In such cases, it may be better to let the molding follow the line of the ceiling.

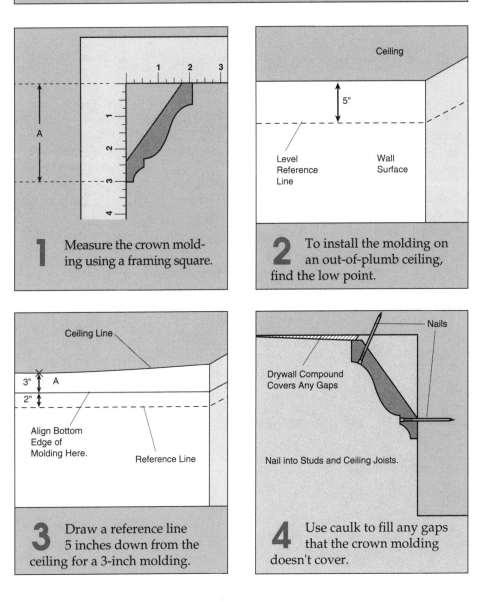

1 Measure the crown molding using a framing square.

2 To install the molding on an out-of-plumb ceiling, find the low point.

3 Draw a reference line 5 inches down from the ceiling for a 3-inch molding.

4 Use caulk to fill any gaps that the crown molding doesn't cover.

Though some people find crown molding difficult to install, it's usually not the joinery itself that causes the problems: all that's needed is a 45-degree miter cut and some work with a coping saw. The tricky part is the way you put the molding in the miter box for that 45-degree cut. Once you've seen it done, however, cutting crown will no longer seem mysterious. To get the hang of it, make some practice cuts on lengths of scrap crown molding first. Even professionals sometimes find this a useful warm-up exercise.

1. Cut and install the adjoining molding. Start by crosscutting a length of crown at both ends so that it fits nicely between opposing walls. Nail it in place.

2. Cut the inside miter joint. Crown molding should be placed in the miter box upside down and backward. That is, the edge that will go against the ceiling when you install the molding should be placed against the bottom of the miter box when you cut it.

3. Cope the miter. Use a coping saw to cut along the profile line created by the saw. The profile line is the front edge of the molding.

4. Check the fit. Hold the coped piece of molding against the piece installed earlier to check the fit. Trim the back side of the molding, if necessary, to make a tight fit, using a file or a knife.

5. Cut the other end of the molding. (A) If the other end will be part of an inside corner, simply cut it square to fit against the opposite wall; the next piece of crown will be coped to fit it. (B) If the other end will be part of an outside corner, place it in the miter box right side up (as it would appear on the wall). Then cut it at 45 degrees. To provide support while cutting the molding, rest its front edge against the saw's fence and hold it securely during the cut.

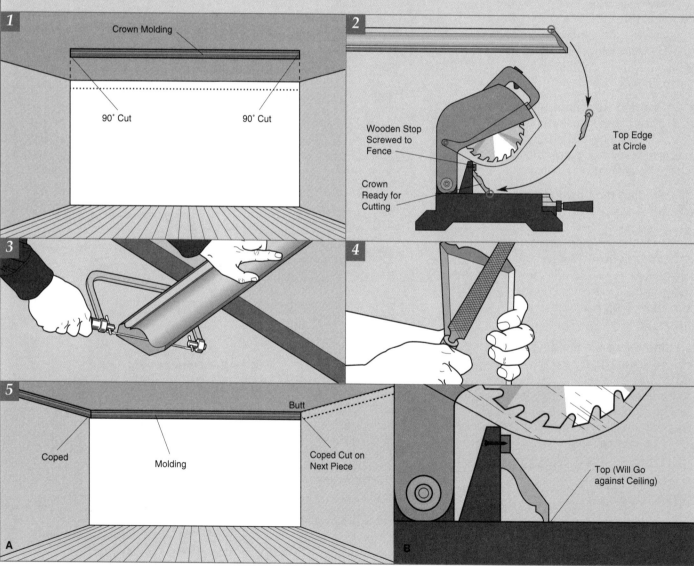

1
Crown Molding
90° Cut   90° Cut

2
Wooden Stop Screwed to Fence
Crown Ready for Cutting
Top Edge at Circle

3

4

5
Coped
Molding
Coped Cut on Next Piece
Butt
Top (Will Go against Ceiling)
A
B

Crown Molding Problems

Cutting crown molding is, in many respects, no different than cutting other profiled moldings. It does, however, present some special problems. For example, if any part of an installed crown molding dips below an imaginary line level, that crown will be impossible to cope. Avoid such profiles, or plan to miter the joints instead of coping them.

Walls parallel to the ceiling joists are often a problem because there's nothing to nail into. One solution is to install blocking at the wall-ceiling joint, as shown, then nail and glue the crown molding to the blocking. Blocking can be made from solid wood or plywood.

When there's no joist or blocking to nail into, you can put some construction adhesive behind the molding (where it contacts the ceiling). Then nail it as best you can until the adhesive grips.

Cutting Cove Molding. The procedure for cutting cove molding is the same as that used for cutting crown. The molding is placed in the miter box with the ceiling edge down so that it can be held firmly in place.

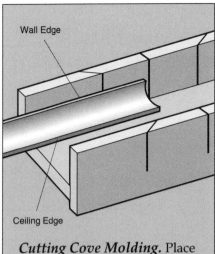

Cutting Cove Molding. Place the molding in the miter box, ceiling edge down.

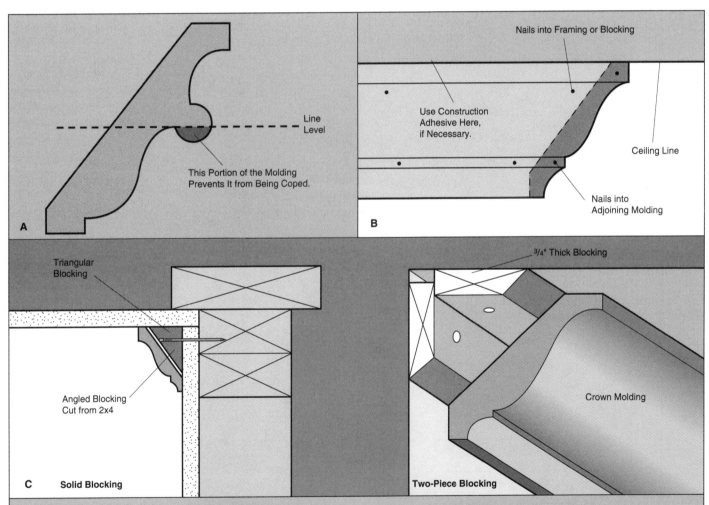

Crown Molding Problems. (A) This crown molding has a profile that cannot be coped. The portion of the molding below the line level shown here would interfere with the cut. (B) This is a typical nailing pattern for crown molding (shown here as a mitered outside corner). If you can't nail into framing at these points and can't provide blocking as an alternative, use construction adhesive to hold the molding against the ceiling. (C) Two methods of blocking behind crown molding are solid blocking and two-piece blocking.

Installing Baseboard Molding

Base trim, including baseboard, is laid out like ceiling molding: by arranging the pieces whenever possible so that each has a butt joint on one end and a cope or miter on the other.

Once you get the feel for installing baseboard, the work goes more quickly. Though all molding should be installed with care, there's a bit more allowance for imperfection in baseboards because they are not nearly as visible as other moldings. You can measure all the pieces before cutting them, or you can hold each one up against the wall and mark where it should be cut.

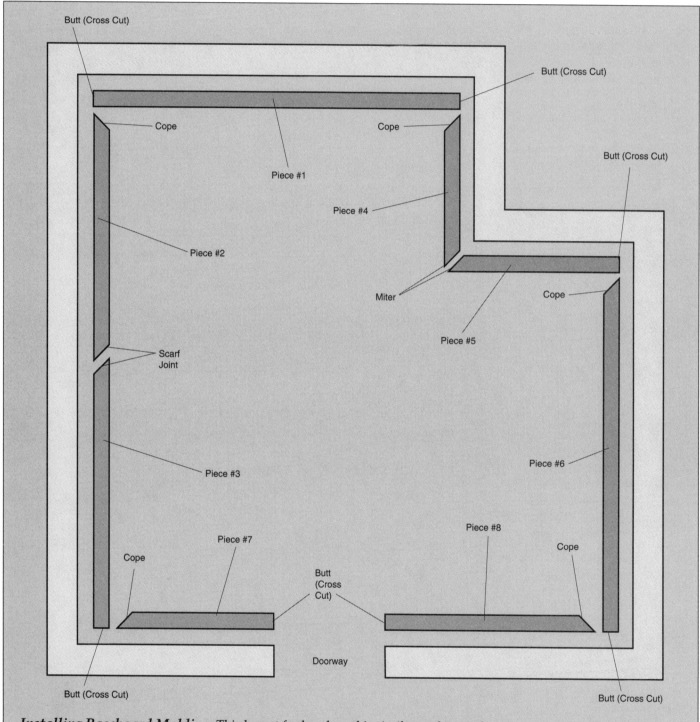

Installing Baseboard Molding. This layout for baseboard is similar to the one for crown molding in the same room. The chief difference is that pieces #7 and #8 will butt into the sides of the door casing. Also, it's more acceptable to have a scarf joint in baseboard because it is less visible than a scarf joint on ceiling molding such as crown.

1 Cutting the Baseboard.
Cut the baseboard to rough lengths and distribute them around the room.

2 Mitering the Pieces.
Start with an outside corner, if there is one. Miter and fit the first piece, then tack it temporarily in place. Cut lengths of baseboard slightly long so that you have to bow them a little to get them into place. This will guarantee tight joints.

3 Tacking the Baseboard in Place.
Work your way around the room, tacking each length of baseboard into place temporarily.

4 Nailing the Baseboard.
After all the baseboards are in place and you're sure they are where you want them, drive all nails home and set them with a nail set.

Types of Baseboards

In most homes, every room has at least a simple baseboard. A baseboard can consist of a single molded piece or a three-part arrangement that consists of a flat section with a base cap on top and a quarter-round base shoe along its bottom edge. Profiled baseboards—such as base cap and base shoe—must be coped at inside corners. Flat profiles are butted.

Single-piece baseboard is relatively easy to install. Built-up baseboard is more difficult, in part, because the base shoe (and sometimes the base cap) is installed after the main portion of the baseboard. They are coped or mitered separately.

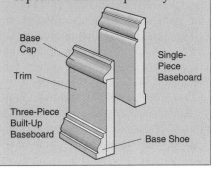

Base Cap

Trim

Three-Piece Built-Up Baseboard

Base Shoe

Single-Piece Baseboard

1 At this point, the baseboard needs only to be cut to the approximate size.

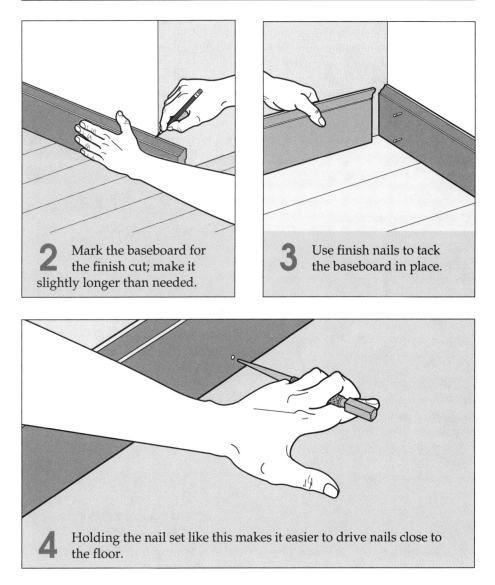

2 Mark the baseboard for the finish cut; make it slightly longer than needed.

3 Use finish nails to tack the baseboard in place.

4 Holding the nail set like this makes it easier to drive nails close to the floor.

Installing Base Shoe Molding

When a floor is uneven, a baseboard may have gaps beneath it in places. A shoe molding is meant to cover these gaps. Because it is slender, it can more easily follow the contours of the floor. Another common use of shoe molding is to cover the edges of newly installed sheet vinyl flooring.

■ Be sure to nail into the baseboard, not the floor.

■ Use the shoe molding to cover slight gaps between the baseboard and flooring.

Fitting Baseboard to Vertical Trim

Where baseboards meet door casings or other vertical trim, you'll have to make accurate butt joints. Though the joint itself is simple, its location near the most traveled part of any room makes it a very visible joint. The best way to mark the cuts is to use a homemade marking gauge made from 1/2-inch plywood. The gauge is notched to fit around the baseboard. Hold it firmly to the edge of the vertical trim, and draw a line on the face of the baseboard using the gauge as a guide.

Making a Half-Lap

Some types of baseboards, particularly those with simple profiles, are awkward to cope because the top edge of the coped piece will be very thin and fragile. One solution is to butt the flat part of the baseboard and miter the curved part. This is called a half-lap miter.

A half-lap miter joint is a combination of several cuts; a miter, a cope, and a butt joint. The joint is time consuming to make, but makes a particularly fine finishing touch on moldings with a full, rounded-over top. Such moldings can be coped, but the curved top sometimes results in a coped joint with a very fine—and a very fragile—top edge.

1 **Mitering the First Piece.** First, use a hand saw to cut a miter

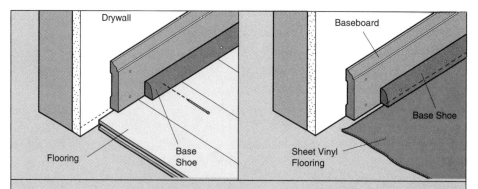

Installing Base Shoe Molding. (A) Fasten the shoe with 4d nails, driving them into the baseboard, not into the floor. (B) The baseboard need not be removed when installing vinyl flooring. Base shoe covers what would be a dirt-catching gap between the flooring and the baseboard.

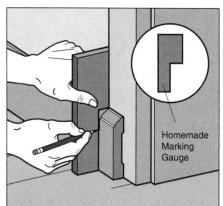

Fitting Baseboard to Vertical Trim. Slip a marking gauge over the baseboard to mark the baseboard cutting locations.

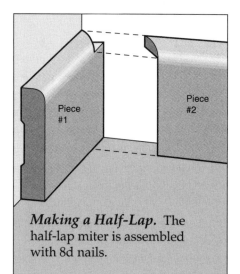

Making a Half-Lap. The half-lap miter is assembled with 8d nails.

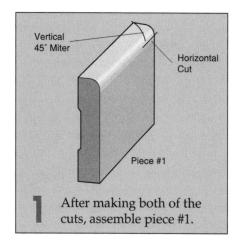

1 After making both of the cuts, assemble piece #1.

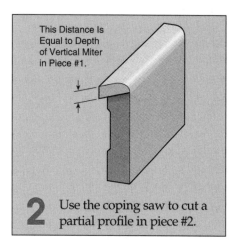

2 Use the coping saw to cut a partial profile in piece #2.

in piece #1 with a miter box; in depth, the cut should stop where the baseboard stops curving. Finish it off with a horizontal cut.

2 **Mitering and Coping the Second Piece.** Then cut a full

45-degree miter on the end of piece #2, just as you would in preparation for a standard cope. But instead of cutting the entire profile away with a coping saw, cut away only part of it.

Installing Wall Molding

Wall and base moldings are relatively common, but wall moldings are less so. This makes them all the more effective when thoughtfully designed and installed properly. Each installation has its own peculiarities.

Chair Rail. As with ceiling and base moldings, lay out chair rail with the outside corners mitered and the inside corners butted and coped. Apart from its functional value in protecting the walls, chair rail is ideal for dividing the wall into sections that can be given separate decorative treatments. For example, you can wallpaper the lower portion of a wall, then cover the exposed top edges of the paper with chair rail. If you also plan to add baseboard after the papering, you won't have to be too precise about the bottom edges of the paper.

Wainscoting. Wainscoting is a decorative or protective wood facing that is applied to the lower portion of an interior wall. In one sense, you could consider it as half-height paneling. Wainscoting comes in a number of styles, and can be as complicated as you wish to make it. There is no standard height, though the top of wainscoting is approximately the same height as chair rail, which is 40 to 48 inches from the floor.

Chair Rail. The proper height of a chair rail is typically 40 to 48 inches from the floor.

Wainscoting. Using wainscoting on a staircase offers protection against handprints and heel marks.

Installing Wainscoting

The easiest way to apply wainscoting calls for tongue-and-groove boards capped with molding. They are available in a variety of woods, depending on regional preferences, but most often they are some type of softwood. The interlocking nature of the boards makes spacing them fairly easy. One alternative to installing wainscoting of individual boards is to use plywood paneling.

1 **Marking Layout Lines.** Mark a level reference line on the wall where you want the top of the wainscot to end.

2 **Cutting the Boards.** Cut the wainscot boards slightly less than the distance from the floor to the reference line. This will accommodate any variations in the floor.

3 **Nailing the Boards.** Nail the boards into place one by one, holding each against the layout line.

Periodically, check the edges of the boards with a level; straighten any that are getting out of plumb.

4 **Completing a Wall.** Start from one corner and work to the next one.

5 **Applying Base Cap.** Cover the top of the wainscot with various base caps or other trimwork, and finish off the bottom with baseboard.

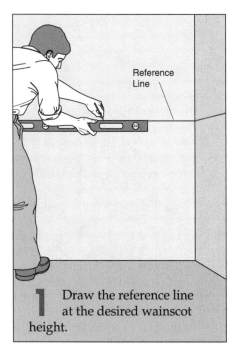

1 Draw the reference line at the desired wainscot height.

2 Cut the boards slightly short, leaving 1/4-inch gap at bottom.

3 Nail through the tongue at the points marked with an "X," then set the nails.

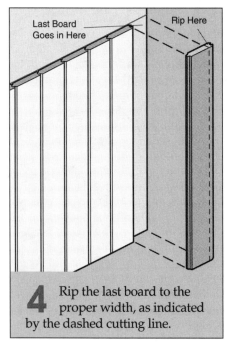

4 Rip the last board to the proper width, as indicated by the dashed cutting line.

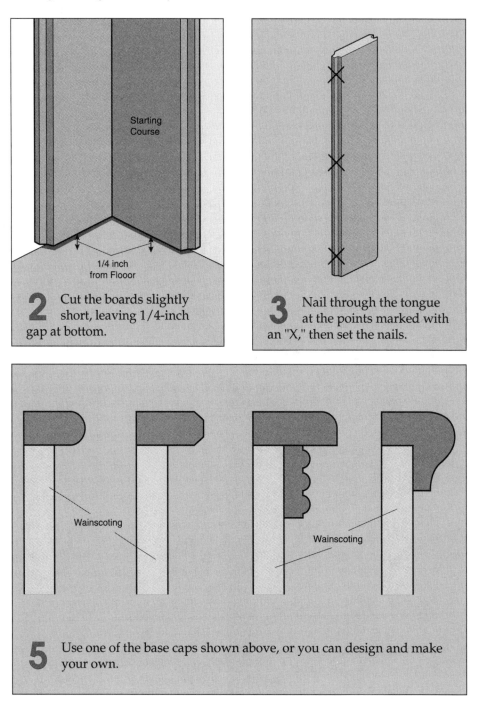

5 Use one of the base caps shown above, or you can design and make your own.

Other Molding

Screen Molding. Screen molding is a half-round or flat profiled molding that's used to protect the cut edges of an insect screen that has been nailed to a wooden frame. Leave the screen a bit long on all sides. After the molding is in place, use a utility knife to trim the screen flush with the molding.

Shelf Face Molding. The edges of plywood or particleboard shelves are usually dressed with some type of molding, whether a half-round, a flat profiled molding, or a simple piece of finish wood. For 3/4-inch thick shelves, nail the facings with 6d nails. For extra strength, add a bead of glue to the back of the molding before nailing.

Corner Guard. Corner guard is used to dress and protect the outside corners of a paneled wall, but it can also be added to drywall corners. It's usually cut with a butt joint on either end to fill vertical space between a baseboard and a ceiling molding.

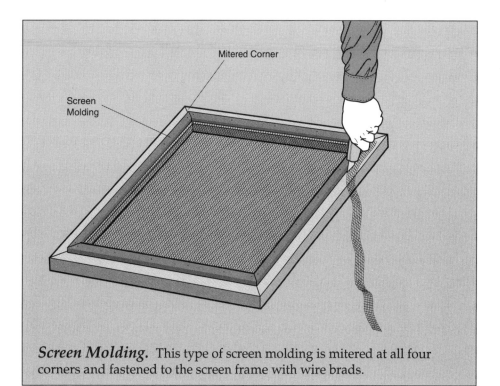

Screen Molding. This type of screen molding is mitered at all four corners and fastened to the screen frame with wire brads.

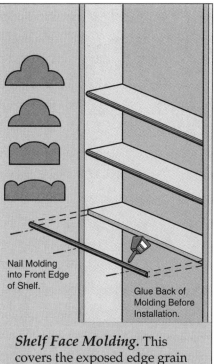

Shelf Face Molding. This covers the exposed edge grain of the shelving, and stiffens it.

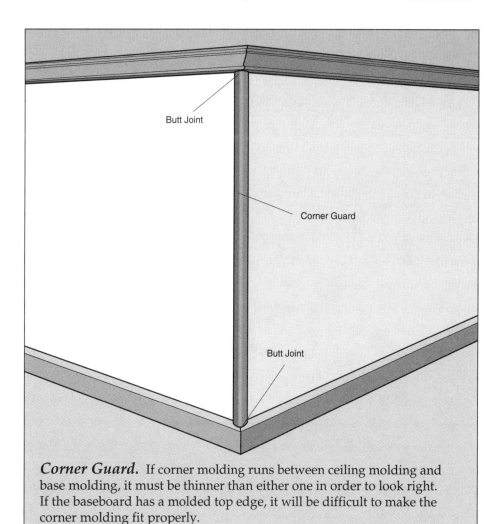

Corner Guard. If corner molding runs between ceiling molding and base molding, it must be thinner than either one in order to look right. If the baseboard has a molded top edge, it will be difficult to make the corner molding fit properly.

Solving Common Problems

Trim and molding are often used to conceal joints inside and outside a house. Indoors, these joints can be found wherever a material changes direction (such as where paneling turns a corner), or where natural wood movement would otherwise create unsightly gaps. Outdoors, trim and molding are often more than just cosmetic. Without them, the many joints between surfaces and materials would invite water infiltration. The resulting leaks are a nuisance, but even more importantly, wood that gets wet repeatedly encourages wood-destroying insects and fungi to attack it. You probably won't be able to see the results of an infestation until considerable damage has been done.

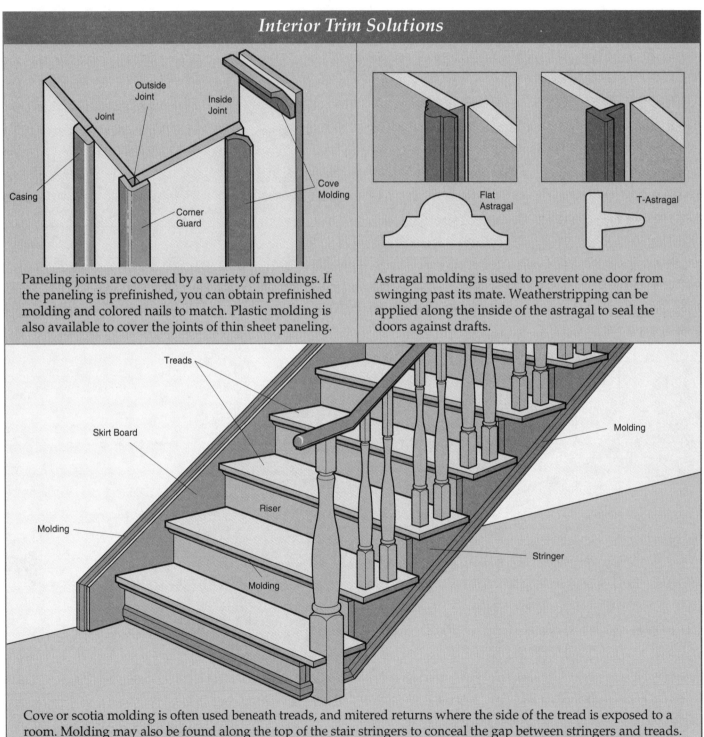

Interior Trim Solutions

Paneling joints are covered by a variety of moldings. If the paneling is prefinished, you can obtain prefinished molding and colored nails to match. Plastic molding is also available to cover the joints of thin sheet paneling.

Astragal molding is used to prevent one door from swinging past its mate. Weatherstripping can be applied along the inside of the astragal to seal the doors against drafts.

Cove or scotia molding is often used beneath treads, and mitered returns where the side of the tread is exposed to a room. Molding may also be found along the top of the stair stringers to conceal the gap between stringers and treads. In the case of open stairs, such as these, molding is used along the underside of the tread, too.

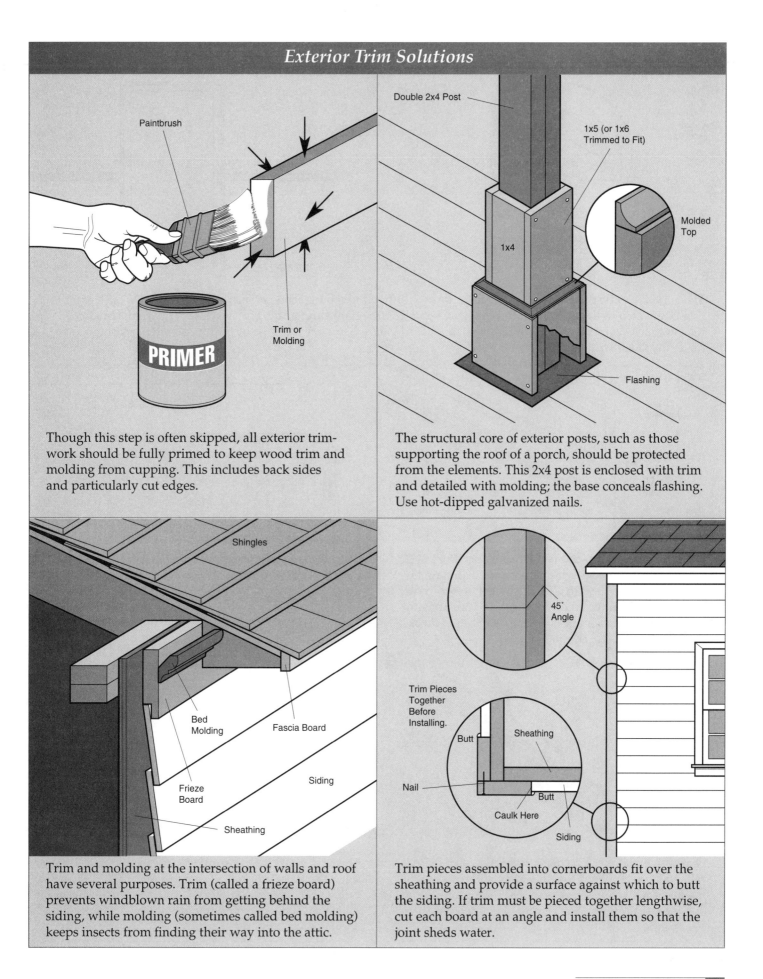

Paintbrush

Trim or Molding

PRIMER

Double 2x4 Post

1x5 (or 1x6 Trimmed to Fit)

Molded Top

1x4

Flashing

Though this step is often skipped, all exterior trim-work should be fully primed to keep wood trim and molding from cupping. This includes back sides and particularly cut edges.

The structural core of exterior posts, such as those supporting the roof of a porch, should be protected from the elements. This 2x4 post is enclosed with trim and detailed with molding; the base conceals flashing. Use hot-dipped galvanized nails.

Shingles

Bed Molding

Fascia Board

Frieze Board

Siding

Sheathing

45° Angle

Trim Pieces Together Before Installing.

Butt

Sheathing

Nail

Butt

Caulk Here

Siding

Trim and molding at the intersection of walls and roof have several purposes. Trim (called a frieze board) prevents windblown rain from getting behind the siding, while molding (sometimes called bed molding) keeps insects from finding their way into the attic.

Trim pieces assembled into cornerboards fit over the sheathing and provide a surface against which to butt the siding. If trim must be pieced together lengthwise, cut each board at an angle and install them so that the joint sheds water.

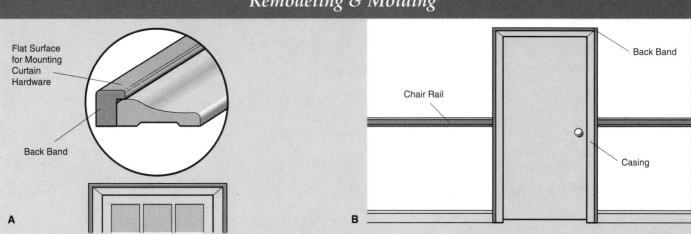

The curved profile of some window casing makes it difficult to mount shade or curtain hardware; (A) back band molding nailed to the casing creates a flat surface wide enough to support the hardware. (B) Chair rail may be thicker than the door casing, resulting in an awkward joint where they meet; instead of replacing the casing, build up its thickness with back band.

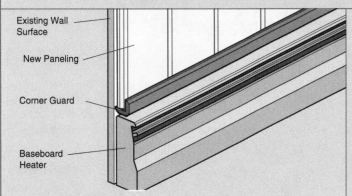

When adding solid wood (usually 3/4 inch thick) paneling to a room that has baseboard heating units, cut the paneling short to clear the heater and trim the opening with corner guard molding. Be sure to maintain appropriate clearances around the heater (check with the manufacturer if in doubt).

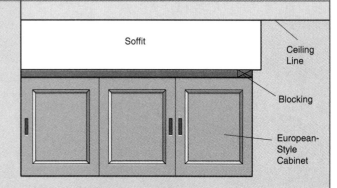

In contrast to standard face-frame cabinets, upper cabinets made with European-style cases must be spaced down from the soffit in order to provide backing for the molding. Blocking can be attached directly to the tops of the cabinets, then the molding can be nailed to the blocking.

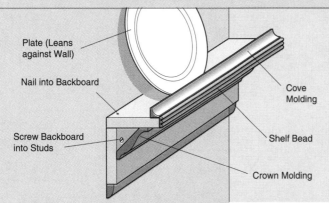

Decorative plates can be displayed safely on a plate rail. Nail top and back together, then add cove molding and shelf bead. Screw assembly through wall finish and into studs, then add crown molding to conceal the screws.

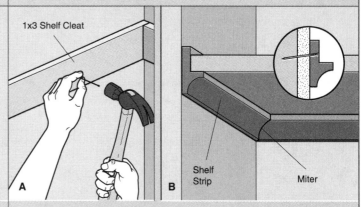

The traditional way to support closet shelving is with a 1x3 shelf cleat (A) nailed into the studs. (B) Molding called shelf strip is sometimes available. It looks nicer than a cleat, but takes more time to install because corners must be mitered.

WINDOWS & DOORS

Whether you are working with windows or doors the techniques required to install trim and molding will be much the same. The results, however, can be anything from simply understated to wildly imaginative. Window and door trim is called casing. Installing casing is an opportunity to showcase your skills while putting the finishing touches on a quality job.

Common Joinery for Windows & Doors

The wood molding around windows and doors is called casing, and it can be installed in all sorts of ways to accentuate a particular decorative style. Generally, the style of the molding (and the joinery used to install it) will be consistent throughout a house. There's no reason, however, not to explore variations on whatever style you choose. In a study, for example, you might want to make the casing more ornate in order to complement other woodwork in the room. In a laundry room, however, you might opt for the simplest casing to save money for more visible rooms.

Nearly all casing installations, however, will use some version of two joints: the miter and the butt. You will never need to cut a coped joint on casing.

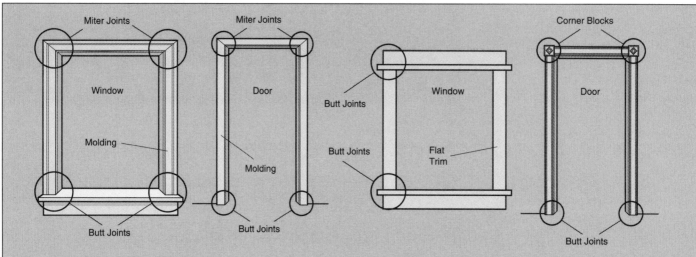

Common Joinery for Windows & Doors. A miter joint is most often used where the side casing joins the head casing. At the sill (on windows) or at the floor (on doors), a butt joint is most common.

Casing Styles

If you walk into different houses around the country, you will probably find mitered casing around the windows and doors (at least indoors; see page 69 for exterior details). This is partly due to economy; this type of casing joinery goes up relatively quickly, and is a part of every carpenter's skills. You can, however, use many other styles. In fact, one of the hallmarks of traditional detailing is the extra care and effort spent upon it.

The casing of a door generally follows the style of any window casing in the same room. When designing the trim detailing for any room, therefore, make sure you consider casing that will look good both on windows and on doors. Sometimes windows can look a little overwhelmed by the same casing that looks terrific on a door.

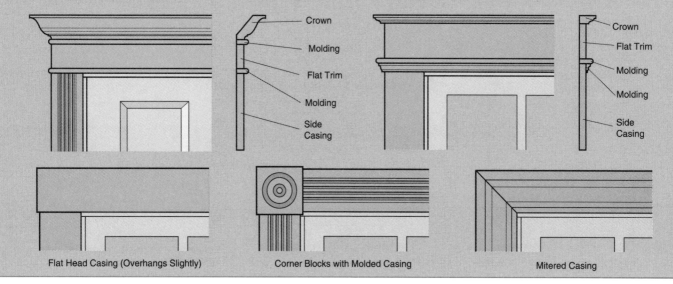

Wall Problems

Casing is nailed to the window or door jamb, and to the wall. In order for the casing to fit properly, however, the edges of the jamb must be in the same plane as the wall surface. In other words, they must be "flush." Any difference between them will show up as a gap.

Testing the Surface. Before installing the casing, run your fingers over the edges of the jambs and wall surface. You can usually feel a difference that you wouldn't notice otherwise.

Filling the Gap. If the difference between them is less than 1/8 inch, any gap that shows up around the casing can most likely be concealed with paintable caulk. This isn't an option, however, if the casing and jambs will be stained instead of painted.

Shaving a High Wall. If the wall is slightly "higher" than the jamb, you can shave it down with a Surform tool. You may want to draw guidelines on the drywall to ensure that you don't remove more than will be covered by the casing.

Trimming the Jamb. If the jamb is higher than the wall, shave it down with a block plane. If you notice the problem before installing the door or window, you may be able to cut down the jambs with a circular saw.

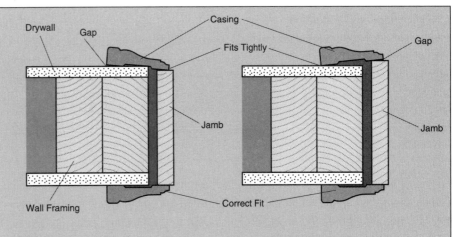

Wall Problems. If the wall surface is not flush with the jamb you will have a gap at one side of the casing.

Testing the Surface. Inspect the jambs and wall surface with your fingers for any gaps.

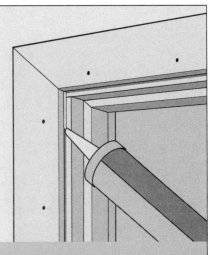

Filling the Gap. Use caulk to fill gaps less than 1/8 inch.

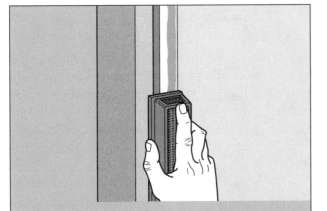

Shaving a High Wall. Remove small amounts of drywall with a Surform tool; coarse-grit sand-paper will also work. Be careful not to damage the surrounding wall surfaces.

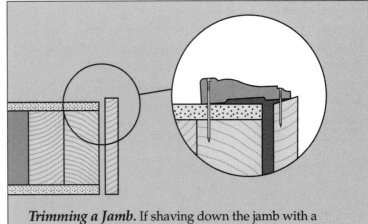

Trimming a Jamb. If shaving down the jamb with a plane, bevel it slightly toward the wall to prevent a gap. Nail only at the outer edge of the casing, nailing in the middle will crack it.

Jamb Extensions

In some cases, the edges of the jamb will fall short of the surrounding wall surface by a considerable amount, and no amount of planing or filing will bring them together. This may be true if your walls are unusually thick. Custom windows can be built to fit the thickness of these walls, but this is very expensive. A better approach is to buy windows and doors with jambs that are not as wide as the wall thickness and then fit them with jamb extensions.

Jamb extensions are wood strips nailed to the indoor edges of the jambs to make up the difference between the jamb width and wall thickness. When ordering windows, order the jamb extensions at the same time, or make your own with a table saw. If planning to stain or use a clear finish on the jambs and trim, the jamb extensions should be made of the same wood as the windows. If painting everything, be sure to use an inexpensive and easy-to-work wood, such as pine, for the extensions. Just be sure that whatever wood you use is straight and relatively clear. Because jamb extensions are so slender, any knots will make them too fragile to work with.

1 Making Jamb Extensions.
Jamb extensions are added after the installation of the window, and are easily made on a table saw. Using this saw will ensure that the extensions are cut uniform.

Caution: *Whenever cutting wood into thin strips, use a push stick or some other method to keep fingers well away from the saw blade.*

2 Installing Jamb Extensions.
Jamb extensions are sometimes installed so that the inner face is flush with the surface of the jamb, but can also be offset slightly. If offset, round off the sharp edges of the jamb before installing the extensions; paint holds better to slightly rounded edges. Use finish nails long enough to penetrate at least 1 inch into the jamb.

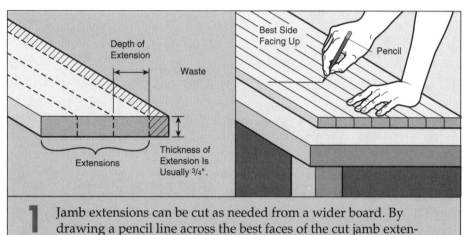

1 Jamb extensions can be cut as needed from a wider board. By drawing a pencil line across the best faces of the cut jamb extensions, you won't install them improperly.

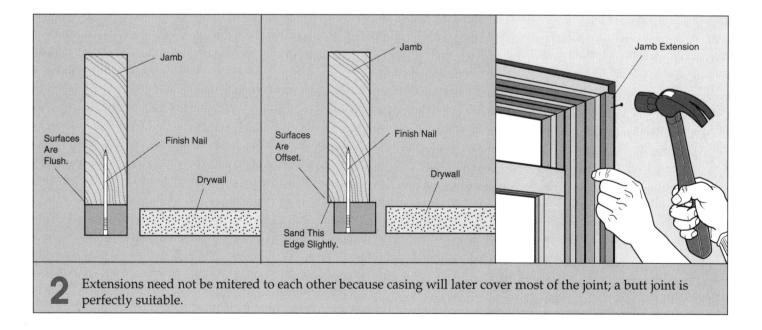

2 Extensions need not be mitered to each other because casing will later cover most of the joint; a butt joint is perfectly suitable.

Installing the Stool

Rabbeted stools have an angled underside that matches angled rough sills, while flat stools match flat sills. In either case, installation is the same.

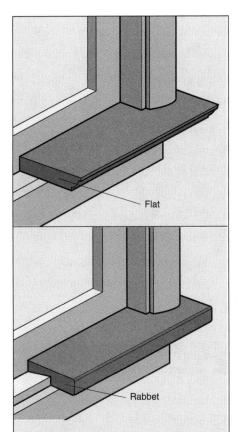

Installing the Stool. The window stool sits against the window sash and on the sill. The stools may be rabbeted or flat to match the sill.

1 Cutting the Stool. First, cut the stool to length. Usually, the "horn" of the stool extends slightly beyond the casing by 1/2 to 1 inch, but this is primarily an aesthetic decision for you to make. Mark the center of the stool, and make a matching mark on the center of the window frame.

Now hold the stool against the window jambs and align the two center marks. To lay out the horns, slide a combination square along the front edge of the stool until the blade rests against one side jamb of the window, and mark the stool as shown. Repeat this on the other side of the stool.

2 Trimming the Stool. While holding the stool against the casing, measure from its inside edge to the sash. Transfer this measurement to the marks just made in the previous step, then draw a perpendicular line from each point to the end of the stool. Cut the stool along the layout lines, using a hand saw or a saber saw. The stool should now fit into place on the window.

3 Nailing the Stool. Round over the edges of the stool with sandpaper before installing it—don't forget to round the ends of the horns, too. Nail the stool into the window framing and set the nails. If the horn of the stool is slender, you can nail through its front edge and into the wall to strengthen it.

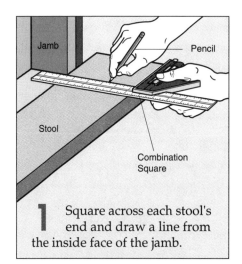

1 Square across each stool's end and draw a line from the inside face of the jamb.

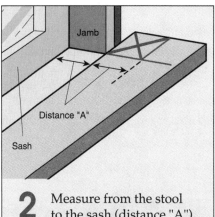

2 Measure from the stool to the sash (distance "A"), then mark out this distance along the line drawn in the previous step. Cut the stool and remove the X portion.

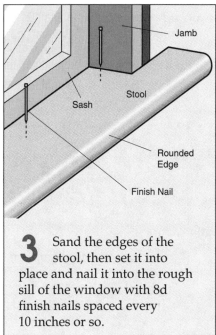

3 Sand the edges of the stool, then set it into place and nail it into the rough sill of the window with 8d finish nails spaced every 10 inches or so.

Trimming a Window

"Trimming out" the window is the last step before painting it. This process calls for installing the stool, apron, and casing (generally in that order). In order for each element to be installed correctly, the pre-vious element must be in the right place.

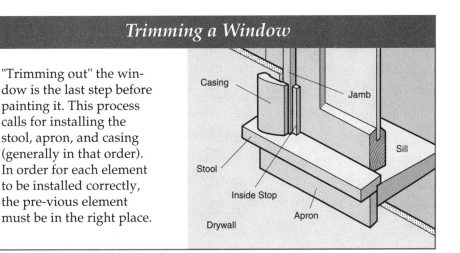

Installing the Apron

The apron is the simplest part of the window trim to install, but even here there's room for a bit of creativity. Decide how long to make the apron and on how to deal with its cut ends. Both decisions are a matter of personal taste.

1 **Cutting the Ends.** Some people prefer the ends of the apron to line up with the outside of the casing, while others would rather the ends fall just short of the casing. The difference between the two amounts to fractions of an inch, but can have a significant visual impact.

2 **Finishing the Ends.** The ends of the apron can simply be cut square and sanded smooth, or finished off with a flourish. Again, it is a matter of personal preference. Experiment with different combinations to see which you like best.

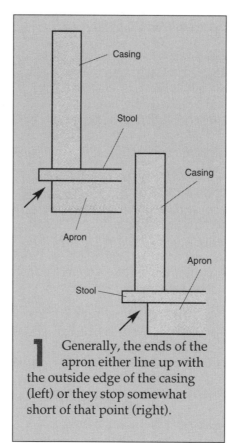

1 Generally, the ends of the apron either line up with the outside edge of the casing (left) or they stop somewhat short of that point (right).

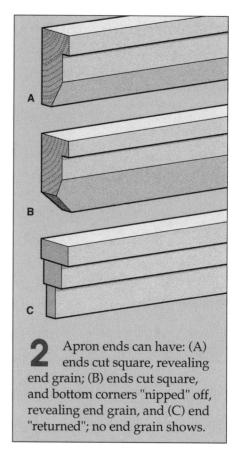

2 Apron ends can have: (A) ends cut square, revealing end grain; (B) ends cut square, and bottom corners "nipped" off, revealing end grain, and (C) end "returned"; no end grain shows.

Cutting a Returned Apron

Of the methods above, cutting a returned apron is most time consuming, but trim carpenters consider it the mark of a first quality job; many others just think it looks the best. This is because the profile on the face of the apron will turn the corner and "return" to meet the wall surface. No end grain is exposed; the ends of the apron are as smooth as its face. The drawings below show how to make a return. Note that these steps must be repeated for both ends of the apron.

1. Cut a 45-degree miter lengthwise through one end of the apron.

2. Cut a mating 45-degree miter in the end of a scrap piece of apron.

3. Place the scrap piece face down on the miter saw and cut off the very end just mitered. This will sever a small, triangular piece of the apron; set it aside for a moment.

4. Nail the apron in place beneath the window stool and glue the small return created in the previous step into place at the end of the apron. Secure the return with small brads, but do so cautiously to avoid splitting the return.

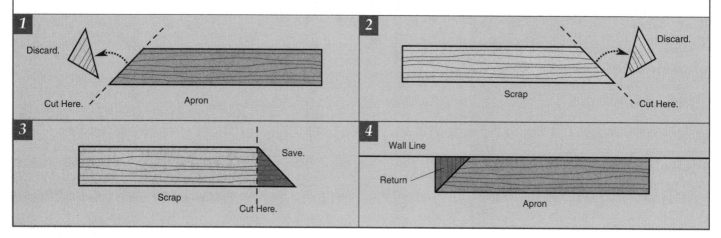

Installing Mitered Casing

Installing window casing is the fussiest part of trimming out a window—any imperfections in the joints will be readily apparent to anyone who cares to look. Though it may take a good bit of patience, especially the first time out, casing a window is not difficult.

1 Marking the Reveals. After you have checked to be sure that the edges of the jamb are flush with the wall, mark out reveals on the edges of the jambs, particularly at the corners. A reveal is a slight offset between the inside face of the jamb and the inside edge of the casing. It's easier to install the casings when not trying to make them perfectly flush with the inside of the jamb, and the small shadow line that results is visually pleasing. To mark the reveals, adjust the blade of a combination square to the size of the reveal and mark the jambs at each corner and at several places along their length. Some carpenters prefer to use a reveal gauge instead of a square. (See "Making & Using a Reveal Gauge," page 65.)

2 Marking the Head Casing. Hold a length of casing against the reveal lines on the head jamb, and mark the base of each miter. Draw a light slash mark on each end of the casing to identify the direction of the miter. (This will prevent you from cutting it the wrong way when you take your stock to the saw.)

3 Cutting the Head Casing. Cut a 45-degree miter on each end of the head casing. The best technique for making any miter cut is to "sneak up" on your layout mark: first, cut just outside of the mark, then adjust the casing as needed to make a second, more accurate cut. Tack the casing in place as you line it up with the reveal marks.

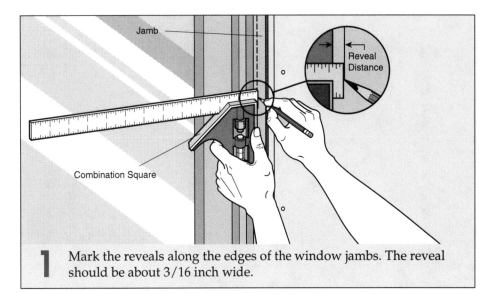

1 Mark the reveals along the edges of the window jambs. The reveal should be about 3/16 inch wide.

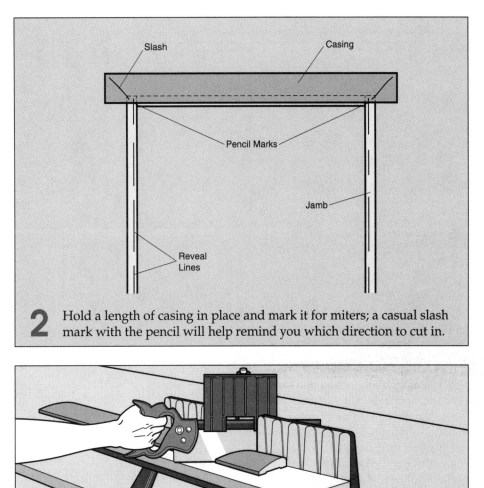

2 Hold a length of casing in place and mark it for miters; a casual slash mark with the pencil will help remind you which direction to cut in.

3 Make a miter cut on each end of the head casing. "Sneak up" on the final cut by making a test-cut first.

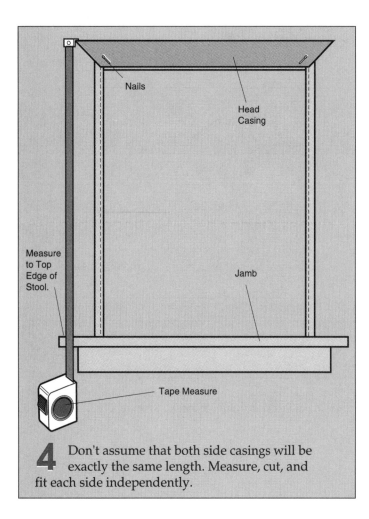

Nails

Head
Casing

Measure
to Top
Edge of
Stool.

Jamb

Tape Measure

4 Don't assume that both side casings will be exactly the same length. Measure, cut, and fit each side independently.

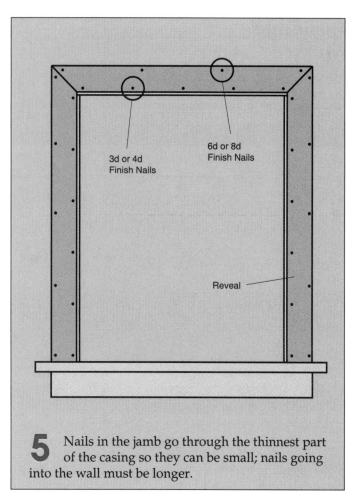

3d or 4d
Finish Nails

6d or 8d
Finish Nails

Reveal

5 Nails in the jamb go through the thinnest part of the casing so they can be small; nails going into the wall must be longer.

4 Marking the Side Casing.
Each side casing will have a miter at one end and a square cut at the other. Make the miter cut first. Then measure from the tip of the head casing to the stool, and transfer this measurement to your stock to provide a cut line for the square cut.

5 Cutting and Fitting the Side Casing. When you make the square cut, make it slightly long—this will allow you some leeway for making a precise fit. Test-fit the casing: line it up against the reveal lines, and cut a sliver off the bottom, if necessary. Tack the casing in place and repeat the procedure on the second piece of side casing. Adjust head or side casings as needed to get the proper fit all around, then drive home all the

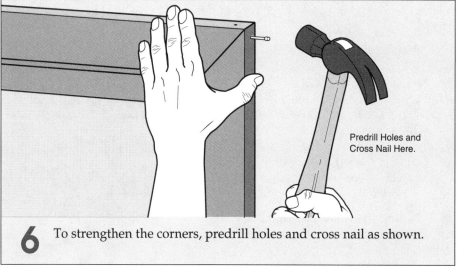

Predrill Holes and
Cross Nail Here.

6 To strengthen the corners, predrill holes and cross nail as shown.

nails. Set them below the surface with a nail set. If you have casing to install on other windows, wait to fill the nail holes until all the casing is done.

6 Strengthening the Corners.
Drill pilot holes through the head and side casings and drive a 4d finish nail through each hole.

Adjusting a Miter

In a perfect world, each miter you make would fit perfectly the first time. But walls aren't always plumb and straight, and jambs aren't always square. When you encounter these situations, your miters won't fit properly unless you adjust them to account for these less than ideal conditions.

Wedging when Recutting. You can change the angle of the saw to recut a miter, but it's quicker to wedge the casing away from the saw fence.

Wedging the Miter's Base. A wedge can be positioned to close a gap at the base of the miter.

Wedging the Miter's Tip. If the gap is at the tip of the miter, the wedge must be positioned differently.

Wedging Behind the Miter. If the miters aren't properly aligned after you recut them, a slender wedge behind the miter will probably even them up.

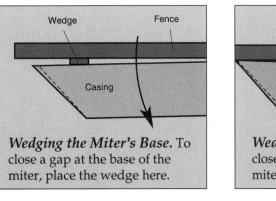

Wedging the Miter's Base. To close a gap at the base of the miter, place the wedge here.

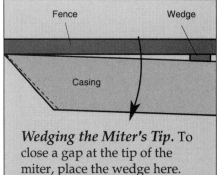

Wedging the Miter's Tip. To close a gap at the tip of the miter, place the wedge here.

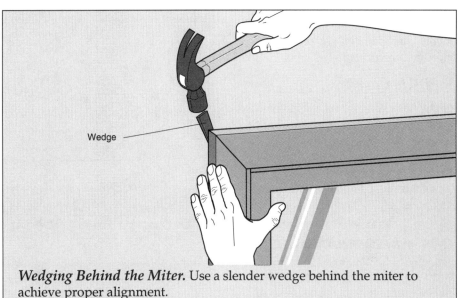

Wedging Behind the Miter. Use a slender wedge behind the miter to achieve proper alignment.

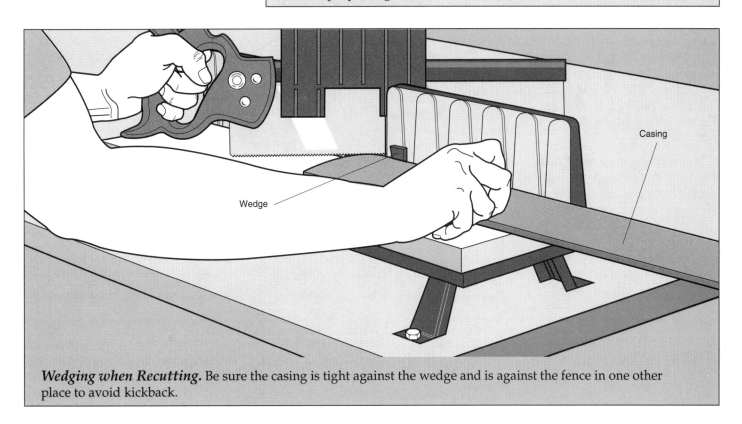

Wedging when Recutting. Be sure the casing is tight against the wedge and is against the fence in one other place to avoid kickback.

Installing
Butt-Jointed Casing

Mitered casing is widespread, but it is hardly universal. Several traditional trim styles rely on an assembly of casing members that entirely eliminate the need for miters. These styles go by various names, but the basic types can be described as built-up casing or corner block casing. Either type can be used on interior doors and windows. Installation calls for laying out the same reveals noted earlier and marking them on the jambs.

Built-Up Casing

Of the two types of butt-jointed casing, this one is the easiest for novices to install. In fact, many find it easier to install than mitered casing because the assembly is more forgiving of minor mistakes in measuring. The casing is usually made from 3/4-inch thick trim stock, rather than molding.

1 Installing Side Casings.
Mark out the reveals on the head jamb and side jambs, just as you would for mitered casing. Then hold a length of casing against one side jamb and mark it at the reveal on the head jamb. (You could measure the distance, but this method is easier and more accurate.) Make a 90-degree cut on the casing at this mark, then nail the casing in place. Repeat the procedure with the opposite side casing.

2 Installing the Head Casing.
The first piece of a two-piece head casing is the same thickness as the side casing, but is narrower. If the casing is 3/4-inch thick, then this first piece can be 7/8 to 1 inch wide, though the exact width is mostly a matter of personal preference. Round over its edges with sandpaper or a router. The second piece of head casing can be nailed to the wall above the first piece.

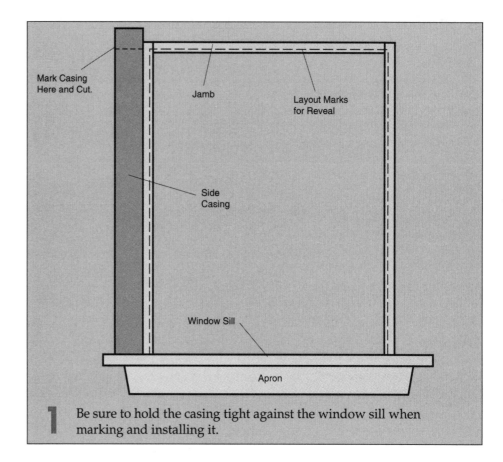

1 Be sure to hold the casing tight against the window sill when marking and installing it.

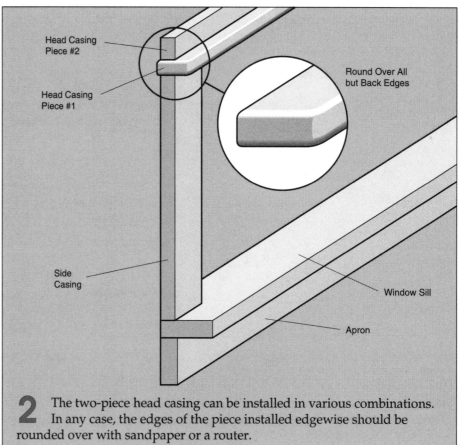

2 The two-piece head casing can be installed in various combinations. In any case, the edges of the piece installed edgewise should be rounded over with sandpaper or a router.

Corner Block Casing

Many Victorian-style houses feature wood corner blocks at the intersections of head casing with the side casings. The decorative blocks can be made on site, but are also available from mail-order suppliers and well-stocked home centers or lumberyards. Head and side casings fit against the corner blocks in a butt joint, rather than meeting in a miter joint. The blocks should be slightly thicker than the casing to conceal the end grain of the casing.

1 Installing the Side Casing.
Mark out the reveals on the head jamb and side jambs. Then hold a length of casing against one side jamb and mark it at the reveal on the head jamb. Make a 90-degree cut on the casing at this mark, then nail the casing in place. Repeat the procedure with the opposite side casing.

2 Installing the Corner Blocks.
Each corner block should sit squarely atop the side casing, with its inside edge flush with the casing's inside edge. Predrill two nail holes in each block and nail it in place. (Predrilling minimizes the chance of splitting the block as you nail it up.)

3 Installing Head Casing.
Measure between the two corner blocks and cut a piece of casing stock slightly longer (no more than 1/16 inch). Fit the head casing in place, and trim it if necessary for a snug fit. The fit shouldn't be so tight, however, that it pushes the blocks out of position.

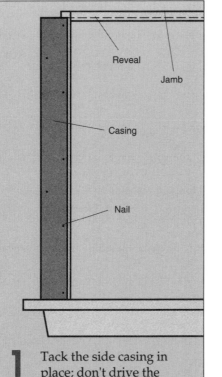

1 Tack the side casing in place; don't drive the nails home until you are satisfied with the position of the corner blocks. This will allow you some leeway for fitting the blocks properly, if necessary.

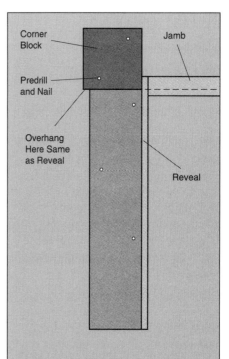

2 The overhang on the outer edges of the corner blocks is usually about the same as the reveal you marked earlier on the jamb, but this is purely a matter of personal preference.

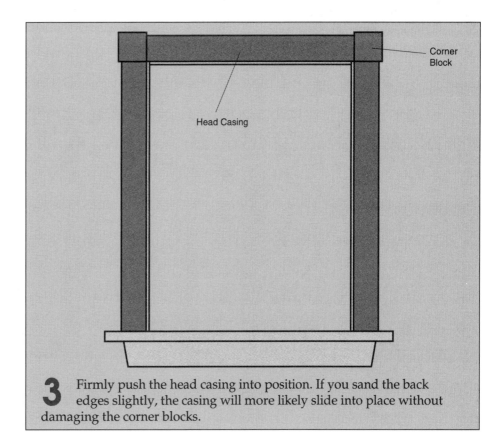

3 Firmly push the head casing into position. If you sand the back edges slightly, the casing will more likely slide into place without damaging the corner blocks.

Installing Picture-Frame Window Casing

Not every window has a stool or an apron. This is sometimes the case with windows that are very high on the wall, or with windows in hallways where the projection of a stool would reduce clearances in the halls. Bay and bow windows are often installed without a stool, too. A lower portion of casing (opposite the head casing) is installed to cover the gap between jamb and wall. This style is called picture-frame casing.

Installing picture-frame casing calls for the same skills required for standard casing, though you'll have to mark reveals on all four jambs instead of just on three. The casing can be installed piece by piece, much as you would install standard window casing. An easier way, however, is to cut and assemble the entire "frame" then install it on the jambs. The jambs must be square to each other; check them with a framing square.

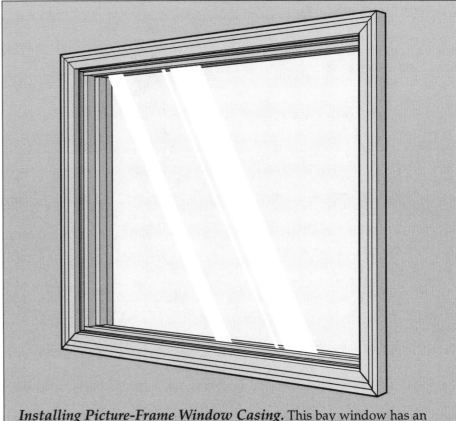

Installing Picture-Frame Window Casing. This bay window has an extra piece of casing where the stool and apron would normally be.

1 **Cutting the Miters.** Lay out the reveals, measure between them to get the casing measurements, and cut all four pieces with a 45-degree miter on each end. Then assemble the "picture frame" face down on a flat surface.

2 **Positioning the Casing.** With all four corners stapled (two in each joint), gently turn the frame over and position it on the window.

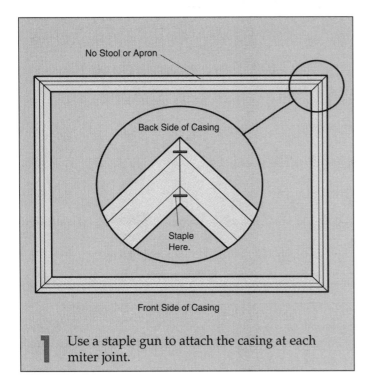

No Stool or Apron

Back Side of Casing

Staple Here.

Front Side of Casing

1 Use a staple gun to attach the casing at each miter joint.

2 Adjust the frame's position to correspond to the reveal marks and nail it into place.

Trimming a Door

Once you've had some experience installing the various trim pieces needed for a window, trimming a door will be easy. A door requires the same measuring process, same reveals, the same miters, and the same nailing sequence. (See "Installing Mitered Casing," page 59.) If your windows required jamb extensions, your doors probably will, too. But there's no stool to install, and no apron. And instead of measuring the side casing to a stool, you measure to the floor.

Note that doors (and sometimes windows) are cased before any other trim elements are installed. This is because baseboards, chair rails, and perhaps even the ceiling molding will butt into the casing. The casing serves, in effect, as a termination point for these other elements.

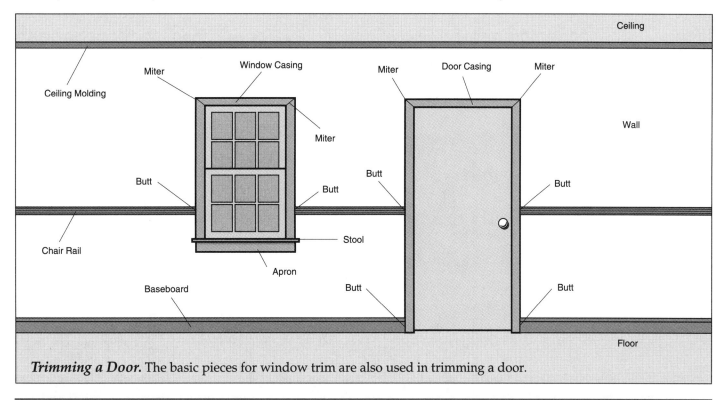

Trimming a Door. The basic pieces for window trim are also used in trimming a door.

Making & Using a Reveal Gauge

Though many people use a combination square to mark out the reveals on doors and windows, a faster way is to use a homemade reveal gauge. The gauge is simply a square of scrap stock with a smaller square screwed to it; the lip formed between the two is exactly the width of the reveal. Using the guide is quicker than using a combination square to lay out the reveals, and will work on any door or window jamb.

1. Start with a scrap of wood that is perfectly square, and use a combination square to lay out the reveals on one face. Then cut a smaller square.

Line up two of the edges of the small square exactly along the layout lines on the large square, then screw the two pieces together.

2. To use the gauge, hold it against the jamb and mark out the reveals. Use a mechanical or standard pencil to mark the reveals.

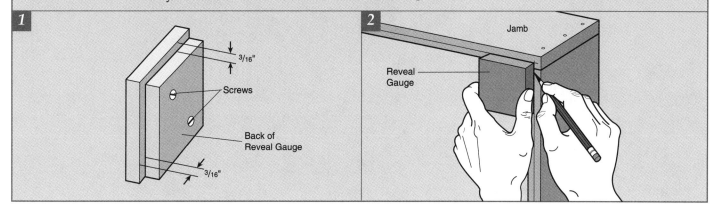

Plumbing Door Jambs

It is particularly important to ensure that the jambs of doors are straight and plumb. This is because the greater length of door side jambs will accentuate any imperfection. Also, door casing is probably the most noticeable trim in a house because everyone walks within inches of it, and at least part of the casing is always at eye level.

A properly installed door jamb should feature side jambs that are plumb and straight, as well as a head jamb that is level. The best way to check the side jambs is with a 4-foot level (you can also use a plumb bob). Hold the level against each jamb and check the plumb vial; if the bubble is centered, the jamb is plumb. However, a plumb jamb isn't necessarily straight, so look for any gaps between the level and the jamb as you hold it in place. If you don't have a long level, use a smaller one and hold it against a long, straight board to extend its "reach."

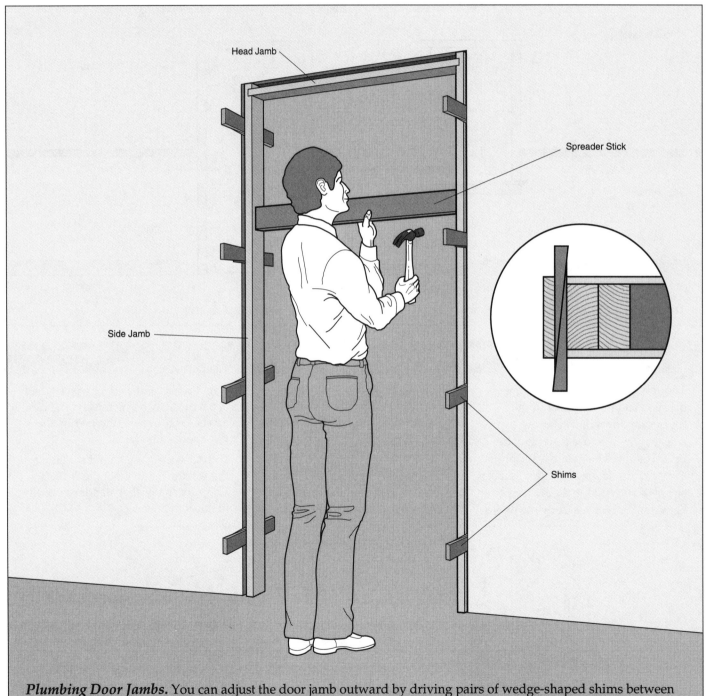

Head Jamb

Spreader Stick

Side Jamb

Shims

Plumbing Door Jambs. You can adjust the door jamb outward by driving pairs of wedge-shaped shims between the jamb and the framing; to adjust the jamb inward, pull the shims out a bit.

Installing Mitered Door Trim

There are several ways to join head casing to side casing around a door. The most common method is to use a miter joint, which is simply two 45-degree angles joined to make a 90-degree angle. You can use other joints, however, depending on your skill and the architectural style of your house.

1 **Marking the Reveal.** The inside edge of the casing should be offset from the inside edge of the jambs by approximately 3/16 inch. The small edge caused by offsetting the two is called a reveal. Set the combination square for 3/16 inch and use it to guide your pencil around the jamb, leaving a line 3/16 inch from the edge.

2 **Making the First Miter.** Cut a length of casing square at one end. Then place the casing against the reveal line, and square cut against the floor. Mark the casing at the point where the vertical and horizontal reveal lines intersect, and cut a 45-degree angle at this point.

3 **Making the Next Miters.** Nail the first piece of casing to the jamb with 3d or 4d casing nails spaced every 12 inches or so. Now cut a 45-degree angle on another piece of casing, fit it against the side casing, mark it for the opposite 45-degree angle, then cut and install it.

4 **Completing the Final Miters.** After installing the head casing, mark, cut, and install the final length of side casing.

5 **Setting the Nails.** After nailing the casing in place, set all the nails just below the surface of the wood, then fill the holes with wood putty and sand them smooth when dry. Use a nail set and a lightweight hammer to set the nails.

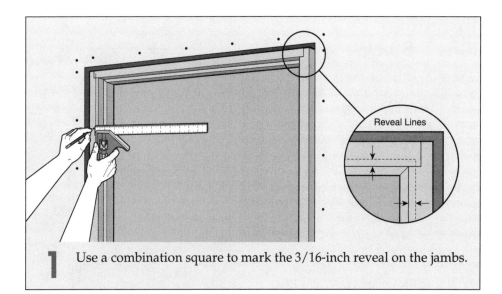

1 Use a combination square to mark the 3/16-inch reveal on the jambs.

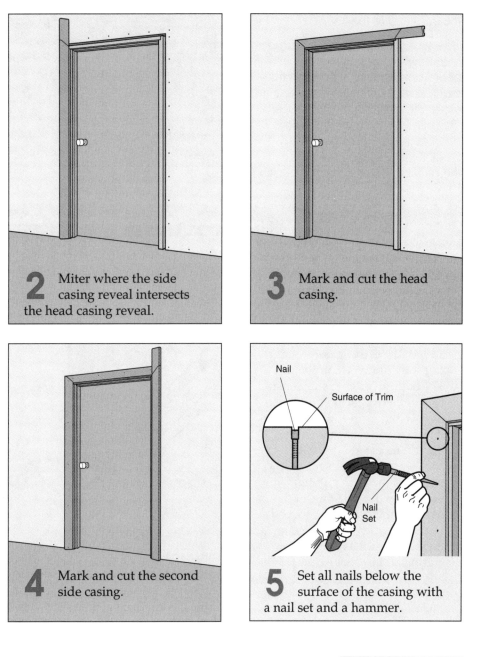

2 Miter where the side casing reveal intersects the head casing reveal.

3 Mark and cut the head casing.

4 Mark and cut the second side casing.

5 Set all nails below the surface of the casing with a nail set and a hammer.

Installing Plinth Blocks

One detail found on some doors that is not found on windows is the plinth block. These decorative blocks provide a transition between casing and baseboard; they are nailed to the bottom of the door jamb and the lower portion of the wall. When a door is trimmed with plinth blocks as well as decorative corner blocks, all the pieces meet with butt joints—there is no need to miter it. Nail plinth and corner blocks in place with finish nails long enough to penetrate well into the wall framing. Generally, 8d or 10d nails will do the job. Countersink the nails and fill the holes.

The door casing butts into the top of the plinth block, while the baseboard butts into its side. A plinth block should be slightly thicker than either the casing or the baseboard. This allows it to conceal the end grain of those trim elements. The block should also be taller than the baseboard for the same reason.

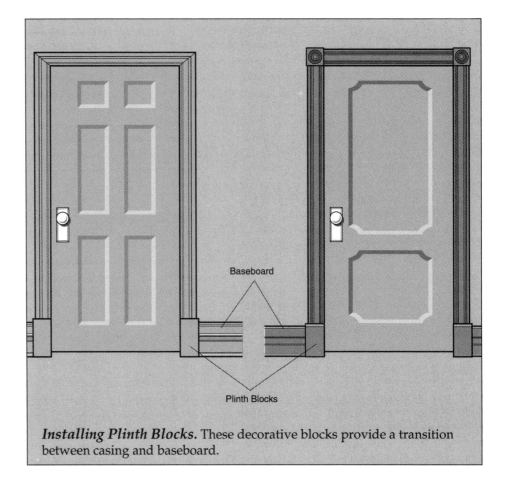

Installing Plinth Blocks. These decorative blocks provide a transition between casing and baseboard.

Trimming Existing Door Casing

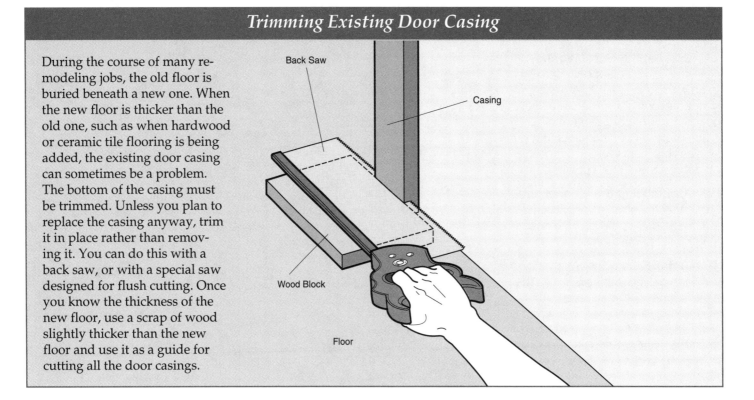

During the course of many re-modeling jobs, the old floor is buried beneath a new one. When the new floor is thicker than the old one, such as when hardwood or ceramic tile flooring is being added, the existing door casing can sometimes be a problem. The bottom of the casing must be trimmed. Unless you plan to replace the casing anyway, trim it in place rather than removing it. You can do this with a back saw, or with a special saw designed for flush cutting. Once you know the thickness of the new floor, use a scrap of wood slightly thicker than the new floor and use it as a guide for cutting all the door casings.

Exterior Details for Windows & Doors

There are several differences between exterior and interior window and door trim. Perhaps the most important difference is that exterior trim is not just there for its good looks: it also helps to keep rain and wind from penetrating the walls. It is very important that you use kiln-dried material. Otherwise, you'll get a lot of gaps at the joints from shrinkage, and the paint may fail as the trapped moisture tries to escape.

When installing exterior trim, take particular care to prevent water from penetrating joints. It is also a good idea to back-prime all trim before installing it, using a good quality primer. This extra step will add years of life to the woodwork. If you plan to paint the trim and siding, be sure to caulk the joint between them well.

Caulking Windows & Doors

After installing any window or door trim, be sure to caulk the outside edges thoroughly between casing and siding. Use a high-quality, exterior-grade caulk. Caulk may be applied before or after the painting is complete. Be sure the caulk fills the joint fully.

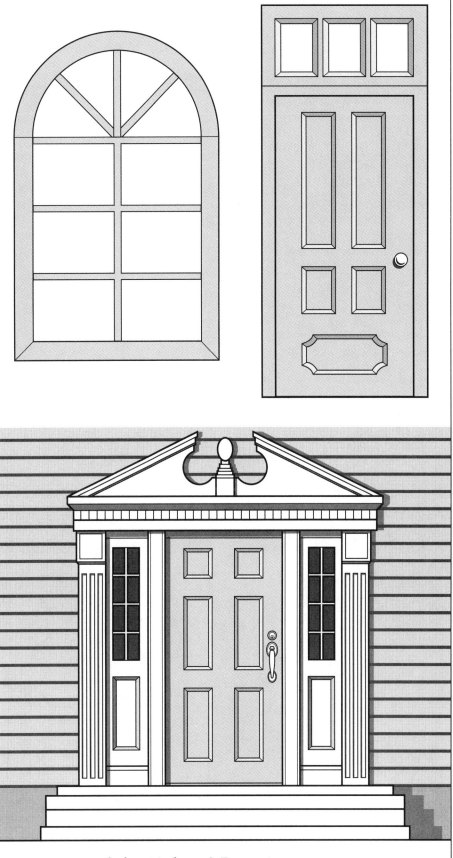

Exterior Details for Windows & Doors. The trim you choose conveys a particular style, as evidenced by the various treatments shown.

Installing Exterior Trim

Casing the outside of a door or window is not very different than casing the inside. The casing is set back from the edge of the jamb by a reveal, head casing is installed with simple butt joints or, sometimes, miters. Galvanized casing nails secure the trim to the window jamb as well as to the wall.

Brick Molding. A type of casing that is unique to exterior work is called brick molding. This is a squarish molding with extra thickness to accommodate various thicknesses of siding. If the brick molding has a decorative edge, side pieces are mitered to the head piece.

Flat Trim. Flat trim, usually 1 1/4-inch thick, is commonly used for exterior casing in situations where brick molding is not used. It is sometimes called "five quarter" trim. Flat trim is particularly appropriate when used with flanged windows and doors; it covers the flange. Some manufacturers recommend that you drill pilot holes through the trim and the flange for nailing purposes; others recommend that you avoid the flange altogether when nailing. Caulk the trim along both edges.

Drip Cap Molding. This detail is not seen as much nowadays. It sits atop the head casing to deflect water away from that joint. It is nailed to the top of the casing with galvanized casing nails, then covered with metal flashing. A drip groove beneath the molding encourages water to drip clear of the jamb rather than seep between the drip cap and the jamb. One reason it is not used as much these days is that many windows feature integral flanges that serve as flashing.

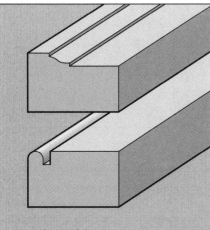

Brick Molding. This casing is attached by manufacturers to the exterior edges of jambs.

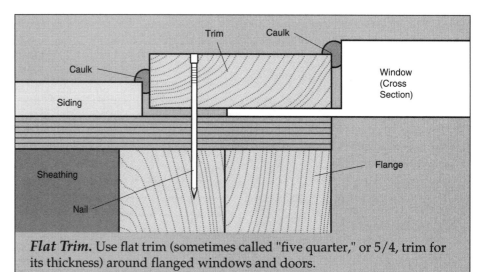

Flat Trim. Use flat trim (sometimes called "five quarter," or 5/4, trim for its thickness) around flanged windows and doors.

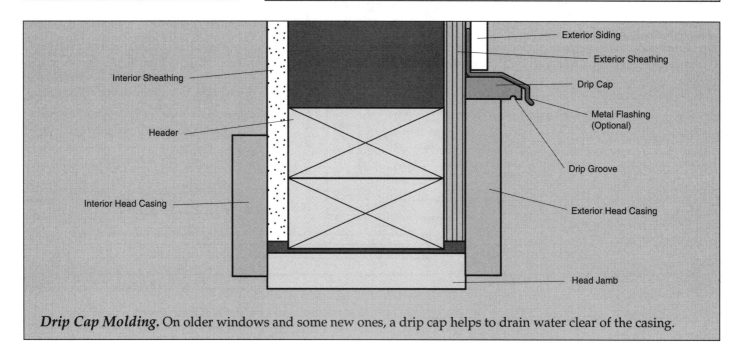

Drip Cap Molding. On older windows and some new ones, a drip cap helps to drain water clear of the casing.

FINISHING & REPAIRING

A finish on trim and molding does more than make the job look better. It also protects the wood and makes it easier to clean. The relentless effects of sun and water lead to damage of exterior trim and molding; left unchecked, the damage will always get worse. To restore the look of the wood, you will have to remove the old finish—or you may have to replace the old finish with new trim and molding.

Before Finishing

The last step in the installation of trim and molding is to fill the holes left behind after setting all the nails. Though this is perhaps the easiest part of the job, it can readily turn into a headache of considerable proportions if you don't follow some simple guidelines.

What aggravates many beginners is the seemingly endless rounds of sanding, filling, and sanding again. It seems as if you're always reaching for the putty knife and wood filler to do a few more holes. The solution is simple: don't fill any nail holes until the entire job is complete and all the nails are set, or you'll loose track of which holes you've filled and which you haven't. There's nothing more frustrating than being up on a step ladder with a paint-laden brush, only to find several small holes that haven't been filled.

While you're filling holes, it's a good idea to scrutinize all the woodwork for small dents and rough areas—attending to them now will save lots of time later on. Dents can be filled with the same material used to fill nail holes; rough spots should be sanded smooth. Rather than try to see these flaws, feel for them. Rub your hand gently over all the trim and you'll find more flaws than you could ever see. Another trick is to shine a strong light across the trim at a low angle; any irregularities will be accentuated by the shadows that they cast.

Filling a Hole

The key ingredient in filling holes goes by various names, including wood putty or wood filler (professional woodworkers use a product that's also called wood filler, but it has nothing to do with filling holes). Whatever you call it, the material is easy to use. Most formulations will accept various finishes, including varnishes and stains. Wood putty does dry out very quickly, however, so keep the container closed whenever you aren't actually dipping into it for more putty.

1. Filling. Choose a putty knife with a flexible, 1-inch blade. Scoop a small amount of putty out of the container, hold the knife at about a 30-degree angle, and force the putty into the hole with a swiping motion. Make another pass across the hole to clear away any excess putty.

2. Inspecting. When the hole is filled properly, its edges can be seen clearly.

3. Finishing. After the putty dries (in as little as 15 minutes), it must be sanded smooth. You can usually tell when putty has dried—it has a lighter color. Power sanding is generally unnecessary if the hole was filled properly; hand sanding does the job nicely.

What to Avoid When Filling Holes

Filling holes is easy once you get the hang of it. After a while you may get so casual about it that you start to use your finger as a putty knife. Don't do it. As your finger passes over a hole, your skin will actually depress the top of the putty slightly, leaving a slight indentation that can't always be sanded flush with the wood surface. If you don't have a putty knife handy, an old credit card works nicely, too.

Another problem that beginners have is putting on too much putty (or, conversely, failing to scrape off enough). Wood putty dries hard as wood and it's no easier to sand. Excessive amounts of dried putty around a hole mean only one thing: you'll need extra sandpaper and elbow grease to get rid of it. You'll find that it is much easier to remove putty before it dries.

Finishing Trim

Sanding. The wood used for trim and molding is typically clear (that is, free of knots) and smooth. But sometimes you'll want to give it an extra going over with 100- or 120-grit sandpaper. The grain of the wood may have been raised slightly by contact with moisture, or perhaps you simply like the feel of ultra smooth wood. Sometimes the surface of trim is marred by marks left behind by the manufacturing machinery used to cut and shape it. These imperfections are called "mill marks" and can be removed by sanding as long as they aren't too extensive. In any case, moldings with intricate details should be sanded by hand to keep the crisp edges from rounding over. But the flat portions of many moldings and trim can certainly be sanded mechanically. Three sanders appropriate for trim and related work are: palm sanders, finishing sanders, and random orbital sanders. When using any of these sanders, wear a dust mask, or connect a dust bag to the tool.

Painting. A good coat of paint, expertly applied, is the perfect finishing touch for any trim and molding. In addition, paint helps to protect the wood from wear and dirt.

Painting Tools

The standard paint roller used to apply paint to walls is hardly suitable for most trim and molding. Its width makes it nearly impossible to maneuver through the intricate details of trim and molding. There are, however, several varieties of trim rollers that can make quick work of intricate painting projects when used in conjunction with brushes.

A good brush, and the right one, is crucial. Disposable brushes are okay for modest touch-up work, but for high-quality trim painting you should invest in a high-quality brush. If you work mostly with oil-based paints, you will also need a supply of paint solvent for cleaning your brushes.

A Chinese bristle brush, made with natural animal hair, is best for applying oil-based paint, varnish, and stain. A synthetic brush is best for latex paint. Use a chisel-edge brush for painting edges; its angled bristles simplify the job. To use this brush, pull it so that the shorter bristles lead the longer ones, and work in long, steady strokes. A trim brush is ideal for reaching into intricate moldings, and it comes in various types of bristles to suit any paint.

Trim and molding are most often painted with a gloss or semi-gloss paint. This makes them easier to clean than is possible with flat paint. It also makes a nice contrast with a wall that is painted with flat paint. There are several keys to a successful painting job.

■ Use long, steady strokes.

■ Apply the right amount of paint. Too much will blanket intricate details and leave runs behind; too little will lead to an uneven appearance.

■ Use paint shields or painting tape to protect adjacent surfaces. Painting tape is a wide paper tape with just enough tack along one edge to stay in place; it strips away much easier than standard masking tape.

Books have been written about the correct methods of painting, and continual improvements both in paint and painting tools make it difficult to generalize about this finish. Your best source of up-to-the-minute paint and painting advice is your local paint-supply store.

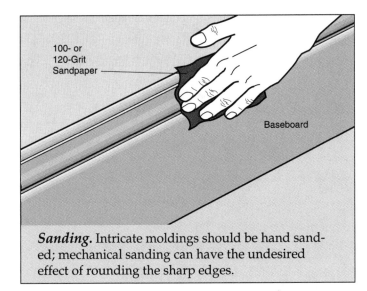

Sanding. Intricate moldings should be hand sanded; mechanical sanding can have the undesired effect of rounding the sharp edges.

100- or 120-Grit Sandpaper

Baseboard

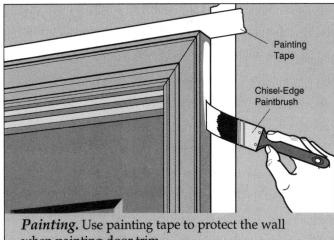

Painting. Use painting tape to protect the wall when painting door trim.

Painting Tape

Chisel-Edge Paintbrush

Repairing Damaged Trim & Molding

If you know how to fill a nail hole, you can repair most of the damage likely to befall trim and molding. Small dents, as well as holes left by removed hardware, are best repaired with wood filler. (See "Filling a Hole," page 72.)

You can also use wood filler to patch larger holes. Start by cleaning away any loose wood fibers or dust. Apply the filler in two passes, letting the first dry completely before applying the second. After the second layer is dry, sand it flush with the surrounding surface, using 100-grit paper. Hand sanding is best because the large area of filler will quickly clog sandpaper used in a power sander. If necessary, square up the edges of the patched area with a sharp chisel. Holes having an open edge, such as the mortise left behind after a hinge has been removed, can be repaired in similar fashion.

If you find that the damage is extensive and deeper than 1/8 inch or so, use an epoxy-based wood patch compound (which is available at hardware and home supply stores) or make a solid wood patch. The wood you use for a patch should match the existing wood as closely as possible.

1 **Cutting the Patch.** Cut an angular patch from some wood scrap. It should be large enough to cover all the damage and slightly thicker than the deepest part of the damage. Trace the shape of the patch on the wood.

2 **Routing the Patch.** Excavate the area by using the router fitted with a straight cutting bit. Then clean up the corners of the excavation with a chisel.

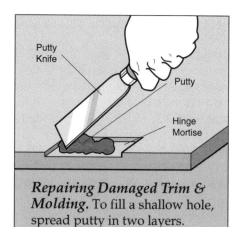

Repairing Damaged Trim & Molding. To fill a shallow hole, spread putty in two layers.

3 **Gluing in the Patch.** Glue the patch in place. Once the glue has dried, sand the patch flush with the surrounding wood.

4 **Finishing the Patch.** Vacuum away all resulting sawdust, then spread wood putty around the perimeter of the patch, forcing it into any gaps. After the putty dries, sand the area smooth.

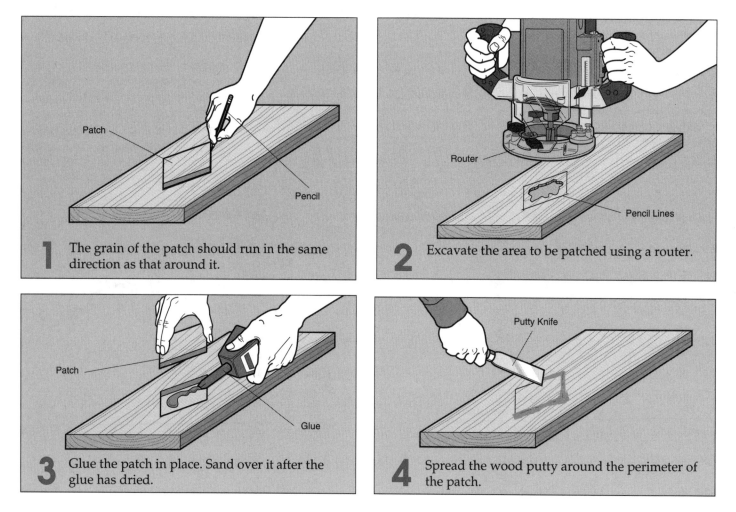

1 The grain of the patch should run in the same direction as that around it.

2 Excavate the area to be patched using a router.

3 Glue the patch in place. Sand over it after the glue has dried.

4 Spread the wood putty around the perimeter of the patch.

Removing Baseboard

1 Removing Base Shoe. First remove any molding, such as base shoe, that is attached to the baseboard. You may find that it's impossible to remove fragile base shoe molding without breaking it, but it is relatively inexpensive to replace. Slip a stiff paint scraper or (better yet) a small prybar behind the molding and pry it away from either the baseboard or floor. (You may have to experiment to figure out which surface it is actually nailed to.)

2 Pulling the Nails. If you can't pry the molding loose with ease, drive the nails through the wood with a nail set and pull them after removing the molding; you can patch the holes later.

3 Prying Loose Baseboard. Baseboard is not nearly as flexible as molding, making it harder to remove but less likely to snap during the effort. Start at one end of the baseboard, ideally where it intersects a door. (You can start at a corner, but make sure you don't try to loosen the butt end of a coped joint.) Then slip a prybar between baseboard and wall, taking care not to damage the fragile top edge of the baseboard. Slip a thin scrap of wood behind the prybar to protect the wall surface, then gently lever the baseboard away from the wall. Don't try to pull it entirely clear; you will crack the wood. Instead, continue down the length of the baseboard with the prybar, opening up a modest gap as you work.

4 Pulling Baseboard Away from Wall. Then go back to where you started, open the gap a bit more, and again work your way down the baseboard. Pry close to existing pairs of nails, rather than midway between them, for best results. With any luck, the entire baseboard will eventually pull away, along with all the nails.

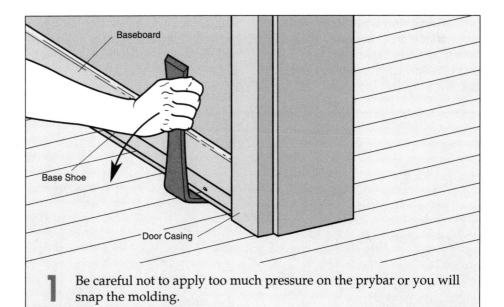

1 Be careful not to apply too much pressure on the prybar or you will snap the molding.

2 If a molding will not pry loose, use a nail set to drive the nails through the wood before removing it.

3 To remove baseboard starting at a corner, remove the coped portion first, then the butt portion.

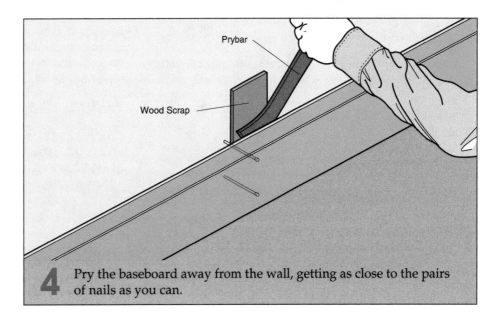

4 Pry the baseboard away from the wall, getting as close to the pairs of nails as you can.

5 **Removing Baseboard with Block and Hammer.** Another way to remove baseboard is to pry it from the wall as just described, but once you've opened up a small gap, use a block and a hammer to pound the baseboard back against the wall. Sometimes the nail heads will pop clear of the base, so you can pull them with the prybar.

6 **Wedging Baseboard.** You can also remove baseboard by wedging it away from the wall. Be sure to use a wood shingle or similar item as the wedge.

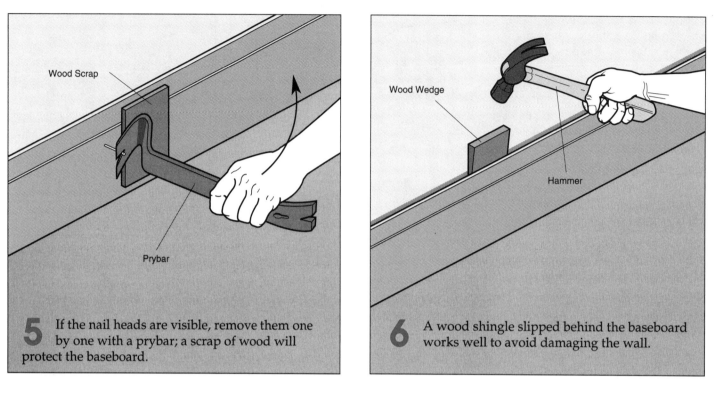

Wood Scrap

Prybar

Wood Wedge

Hammer

5 If the nail heads are visible, remove them one by one with a prybar; a scrap of wood will protect the baseboard.

6 A wood shingle slipped behind the baseboard works well to avoid damaging the wall.

Removing Trim & Molding

You may be able to patch a length of trim or molding, but sometimes nothing short of replacement will do. This is true if the damage is extensive, such as where rot or insect damage has a long head start on a length of exterior corner trim. Another reason to replace trim is to avoid a time-consuming process of stripping layers of paint that have accumulated over the years.

Before replacing any trim, however, ask yourself a few questions before you reach for your tools:

■ Is the trim old? If so, you may not be able to match adjoining trim exactly in width and profile. This might not be a problem if all the casing in a room is going to be replaced, however.

■ Is the trim made of hardwood? Hardwood trim commands a premium price, so you face considerable expense if you plan to replace your old hardwood with new hardwood. This is a case where even a big stripping job may be worth the effort. If the wood is painted, scrape a small portion of the paint away from an unobtrusive place to see the bare wood.

■ Is the trim curved? Replacing the curved head casing over an arch-top window can be expensive and time consuming, and usually justifies the effort spent repairing damage.

Caution: *Stripping paint when remodeling can be a health hazard. Older paints may contain lead, and sanding them releases lead-laden dust into the air. Such dust can be highly toxic, particularly to children. Always have your paint tested for lead if you have a lot of it to remove.*

Removing Door & Window Casing

You can often remove casing just as you would baseboard—by gradually prying it loose with a prybar. But you may find a need for additional techniques, particularly when it comes to removing exterior trim. That's because exterior trim is thicker (typically 1 1/4 inch thick) and wider than interior trim and may be held with galvanized nails, which won't give up without a fight.

Cutting Nails. If you can't pry the casing loose, you may be able to cut the nails instead, particularly when it comes to door and window trim. Slip a hacksaw blade between trim and jamb to cut through each nail shank. After removing the casing you can either extract the remaining shanks with nippers or simply pound them further into the jamb.

Removing Assembly Nails. Cornerboards are usually nailed together before they're nailed to the wall, so you may have to remove the assembly nails before you can pry each board away from the wall.

When you remove trim and molding, there's a good chance that the nails will still be attached. If you aren't going to reuse the wood, bend back the nails to minimize any accidental scratch or puncture wounds, and dispose of the trim promptly. If you plan to reuse the wood, the best way to remove nails is to pull them through the wood from the back side using nippers or side cutters. Pounding them back through the wood is likely to splinter it, and exposes a hole that has to be patched. Grasp the shank of the nail with one edge of the nippers and lever the nail out.

Pulling Nails. Another way to remove trim, particularly if you can't reuse it anyway, is by driving the claws of a nail puller into the wood to reach the head of a countersunk nail.

Place the tip of the puller's claw adjacent to a nail head. Strike the back of the puller with a hammer to drive the claw at an angle into the wood; you may have to try several times. Then use the puller as a lever to remove the nail. This will result in some damage to the wood, so use this technique only if you plan to replace the removed trim with new trim.

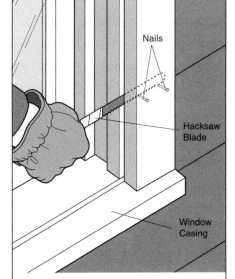

Cutting Nails. Use heavy tape, or a plastic handle, to protect your hands from the saw blade, and wear gloves as well.

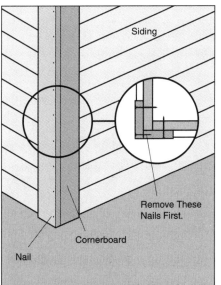

Removing Assembly Nails. To remove assembly nails such as those shown here without damaging the cornerboards, use a hacksaw to cut them.

Pulling Nails. A nail puller driven into the wood enables you to remove nails that have been countersunk.

Recognizing Rot & Insect Damage

Relentless cycles of wetting and drying, 100-degree temperature swings, the corrosive effect of salt air—the outside of a house is a tough place for any material. Wood, however, has additional enemies, including insects and fungi (a fungus is essentially a plant with no leaves that gets nutrients from organic matter such as wood). Trim and molding used indoors is unlikely to be attacked, but outdoors the story is different. Likely locations for problems include anywhere wood is close to the ground, including the bottoms of door casing and corner-boards, skirt boards, and any trim around decks.

Prevention and Diagnosis. Wood-destroying fungi and insects all require about the same basic conditions to thrive, though in various measures: oxygen, favorable temperatures, a food source, and moisture. If you eliminate any one of these essentials, you make it that much more difficult for the organism to survive. Of these factors, it's generally easiest to remove the source of moisture by caulking joints, keeping wood well away from earth contact, and ensuring proper ventilation. Chemical treatments of wood can remove it as a food source, but application should generally be left to professionals.

There are several ways to determine if you might have a problem. You may be able to see the clues, but if not, tap the wood with a hammer and listen for the dull thud indicating interior damage. If you can stick a standard screwdriver even part-way into the wood without much effort, the wood may be infested with insects or fungi. Call in a professional to determine the best course of treatment.

Enemies of Wood

Name	Damage	How to Recognize
Brown rot	Strength of wood decreases rapidly. Most common fungi in houses.	Wood dark brown and crumbly; breaks into small cubical pieces.
White rot	Strength of wood decreases slowly. Most common on hardwoods	Wood looks bleached, feels spongy, has black lines running throughout the bleached area.
Soft rot	Wood softens increasingly from surface inward. Occurs where wood exposed to moisture for long periods.	Similar to brown rot.
Mold	Doesn't harm wood directly, but increases moisture permeability of wood that encourages growth of decay fungi.	Darkened areas on the wood surface, often black, green or yellow. If discolored wood feels dry, fungus is probably inactive. Can grow on or through a paint film. Most likely on shaded portion of house. Staining can be removed by bleaching or light sanding.
Subterranean termite	Most destructive insect. Feeds on cellulose in wood, but damage difficult to see from surface even when infestation is severe.	Nest in the ground but will travel up to 40 yards to a feeding source. Most common sign of infestation is a swarm of winged termites congregating on portion of house. Also look for feeding tubes that lead from ground to wood.
Carpenter ant	Does not eat wood, but tunnels through it while nesting.	Look for swarming outdoors in Spring, or indoors any time. Look for small piles of sawdust near infestation.
Powderpost beetle	Attacks only hardwoods (oak firewood is a common source of indoor infestation).	Leaves small, extremely fine piles of sawdust near infested wood. Attracted to light, so may be found on window sills in infested rooms. Leaves small holes that look as if drilled with 1/32 to 1/8-inch drill bit.

Apron The piece of trim at the bottom of a window, below the stool.

Back band Molding used to decorate the outer edges of flat casing. It can also be used as a base cap.

Baseboard Sometimes called base molding, baseboard protects the lower portion of the walls, and covers any gaps between the wall and the floor.

Base cap Molding applied to the top of baseboard molding.

Base shoe Molding used to conceal any variation between the floor and base-board bottom. It is also used to cover edges of sheet vinyl flooring (when installed without first removing baseboard).

Biscuits Football-shaped pieces of compressed wood glued into slots that have been cut into the pieces of stock that will form a joint.

Blocking Wood stock toenailed between or adjacent to studs to give you a solid surface to nail the molding into.

Built-up molding Several profiles of molding combined to appear as one large piece of molding. Most often it is used as ceiling molding or on the exterior of the home.

Butt joint Two pieces of wood joined at their square cut ends.

Casing The trim that is used to line the inside and outside of a doorway or window frame.

Chair rail Molding installed at a height that protects walls from being damaged by chair backs. It is also used to cover the edges of wainscoting.

Clear grade A grade of lumber or molding that has no knots or other visible defects.

Compound miter A cut that angles in two directions simultaneously.

Coped cut Made with a coping saw, this curved cut is made on a piece of molding with a 45-degree mitered face.

Coped joint A curved cut made across the grain of molding that makes a reverse image of the piece it must butt against.

Corner guard Molding that protects the outside corners of drywall or plaster in high-traffic areas.

Cove Molding that covers the inside corners between sheets of paneling. I t is also used for built-up crown molding.

Cross-cut A straight cut that runs across the grain of the wood. Since the grain of trim and molding runs along the width of the wood, a cross-cut would be made across the width of the trim and molding.

Crown Molding that is used for a dramatic effect at the juncture of walls and ceilings.

Half-lap miter joint A joint that combines miter, cope and butt cuts. Half-lap miters are used for moldings with full, rounded-over tops.

Jamb The inside surfaces of a window or door opening.

Miter cut A straight cross-grain cut made on an angle other than 90 degrees.

Mitered return Used to continue the profile of a molding back to the wall when the molding does not meet another piece of molding.

Miter joint Straight cuts made on an angle across the grain of two pieces and joined at an inside or outside corner.

Molding Thin strip of wood that has a profile created by cutting and shaping.

Mullion casing Center trim that is used between two or more closely spaced windows.

Paint-grade Molding made of many small pieces of wood joined together into one long piece, using glue and interlocking joinery.

Picture rail Molding used to hang metal hooks to suspend paintings and wall hangings, so there is no need to put holes in the wall.

Plumb Vertically straight, in relation to horizontally level surface.

Reveal Amount of the jamb (usually 3/16 inch) that is allowed to show at the edges of the casing of a window or door.

Rigid polyurethane molding Trim and molding extruded into various profiles. It is lightweight, stable, and paintable.

S4S Stands for "surfaced for sides." Designates dimension lumber that has been planed on all sides.

Sash The framework into which window glass it set. Double-hung windows have an upper and a lower sash.

Scarf joint A 45-degree miter cut across the grain that is used to join lengths of molding end to end.

Screen molding Half-round or flat molding used to protect the cut edges of screening nailed to a wood screen door.

Shelf molding Molding that covers the exposed edges of plywood or particleboard casework and shelving.

Shims Thin wood wedges used for tightening the fit between pieces, such as filling the gap between the window and sill when installing a window.

Stool The piece of window trim that provides a stop for a lower sash and extends the sill into the room.

Stops Narrow strips of wood nailed to the head and side jambs to prevent a door from swinging too far when it closes. They also keep the window sash in line.

Stud Vertical member of a frame wall, usually placed at either end and every 16 inches on center.

Trim Unmolded strips of wood used alone or in combination with molding.

Wainscoting cap Molding used to cover the exposed end grain on solid wood wainscoting.

Wainscoting Paneling applied to the lower half of an interior wall.